T0162262

The Nᴛʜ Reader

The NTH Reader

Neglected Texas History

Charles Chupp

REPUBLIC OF TEXAS PRESS

Dallas • Lanham • Boulder • New York • Toronto • Oxford

Published by Republic of Texas Press
An Imprint of the Rowman & Littlefield Publishing Group
4501 Forbes Boulevard, Suite 200
Lanham, MD 20706

Distributed by National Book Network

Library of Congress Cataloging-in-Publication Data

Chupp, Charles, 1929–
   The NTH reader : neglected Texas history / Charles Chupp.
     p. cm.
   ISBN 1-55622-944-5 (alk. paper)
   1. Texas—History—Humor. 2. Texas—History—Anecdotes. I. Title.
  F386.6 .C49 2003
  976.4—dc21   2002010242

Manufactured in the United States of America.

In Memoriam: Marjorie Morris and George Dolan
A pair to draw to.

Contents

Foreword   xi

Preface   xv

Alpha A   Daring the Barren Bering   1

1   Much Obliged   7

2   Traditional Tribulation   9

3   San Saba Silver   13

4   Moses and Son   17

5   Fredonia Misfire   21

6   Sam Served   23

7   First Fall of the Alamo   27

8   The Price of Independence   31

9   Sam's Birthday 1836   37

10 Super Brawl   41

11 The Yellow Rose   47

12 Neuces Nuisance   51

13 High and Dry   59

14 Royal Flush   61

15 Lean Library   65

16 Bluecoat Texan   67

17	Tailored Texas	71
18	Taxing Tale	73
19	A House Divided	75
20	Springtime in Luckenbach	77
21	Hog Wild	81
22	Ma Knew Best	85
23	Pass the Biscuits, Pappy	89
24	The Four-Bit Governor	91
25	Jekyll-Hyde Governor	93
26	Medicinal Purposes	95
27	Langtry Legend	97
28	Hanging Out	99
29	Pike's Pique	103
30	The First Fifty	107
31	G.T.T.	111
32	The Democratic Way	117
33	Catalostrophic	121
34	Look! Up in the Sky!	125
35	Hell's Half-Acre	129
36	Rakin' It In	133
37	One-Eyed Eagle	137
38	Packing Heat	141
39	No Beef from Joe Loving	143
40	The Maverick President	147
41	Emigrant Legend	151
42	Woe in Waco	157
43	Postscript from Garza	165
44	Holy Ground	167
45	Old Rip	169

46	Doing Hard Time	173
47	Texas's Centennial	179
48	Tiger	185
49	Weathering the Worst	187
50	Unbroken Circle	191
51	Happy Got Lucky	193
52	Bats and Balloons	197
53	Torero-ette	201
54	Outlying Settlements	205
55	High Falutin' Evolutin'	209
56	Tale of Two Cities	211
57	Interred in Style	215
58	Puttin' Al Down	217
59	Town Renown	219
60	Interplanetary Alliances	223
61	Around the Globe	225
62	Close Call	229
63	The Mother of All Texas Festivals, 1521	233
	Omega Ω *The Beat Goes On*	241
	Aftword	245

Foreword

For openers, I hereby proffer my credentials for your astonishment and admiration.

First off, I am a direct descendent of Adam and Eve and claim Noah or one of his three boys and wife as ancestors.

You'll recall how the Good Lord watched from his box seat as Adam and Eve, aided and abetted by their numerous begets, set about the task of populating the Earth, and how He became sorely vexed as He beheld their tacky conduct. His displeasure was of such magnitude that He decided to just call it a crop failure and made up his mind to drown 'em and go to plan B.

He'd taken a shine to Noah's family, so He instructed him to lay a keel and build a boat before the flood. Which Noah did and loaded it with the raw materials necessary for a second stab at establishing a more orderly planet once the rain let up.

When the weather cleared up, the excess water was bunched at the poles and put in cold storage. Noah released the animal pairs, and he, his sons, and the wives went back into action to repeople the planet.

A narrow strip of real estate, which we identify as the Bering Strait, appeared betwixt Asia and Alaska, making it possible to walk across, and a goodly number of Noah's descendents did. Just prior to some ice cap melting, which converted the Strait back into ocean bottom.

Once those adventuresome souls reached Alaska, most of them opted to drift south where the weather suited their clothes and the kids could go barefoot. Naturally, many of them wound up in the area we now know as Texas.

They settled in, set up housekeeping, and assumed they'd found their piece of the rock, but they did not buy title policies.

Meanwhile, Christopher Columbus managed to beguile Queen Isabella over in Spain and smooth-talk her into financing a voyage of discovery. Isabella smooth-talked King Ferdinand, and the deal was done.

Columbus, upon his return, claimed he had discovered a route to India, and he gained the accolades of the civilized world. A mass migration of adventurers and malcontents struck out for the new country and assembled along the East Coast, but they didn't seem to realize or care that the folk they found there might be relatives.

Spats ensued; the newcomers began claim jumping, and warfare upon the early residents and sent them scurrying to the heartlands.

My maternal grandparents loaded their young 'uns into a wagon and struck out for Texas in the 1800s, thereby lowering the census in Water Valley, Mississippi. My dad's father saddled his horse in South Carolina and pointed him west around the same time and made a solo one-way trip, but nobody ever told me why.

Grandpa Brownlee, of English derivation, was paired up with a descendent of the Bering Strait entrants, and Grandpa Chupp negotiated a mate of Germanic roots like unto himself. That mixture, of course, probably put me smack in jeopardy of being earmarked as a mongrel.

Anyway, Hugh Chupp and Thelma Brownlee tied the knot in 1927 and produced me in 1929. My grandparents told me, in strict confidence, that I was without question the most outstanding embellishment to the family tree in all recorded history.

My parents were not nearly as lavish—they either blamed the big depression on me, or perhaps the depression for me. I stuck to them like mistletoe to an elm tree until I managed to gain custody of a high school diploma.

At that juncture, Hugh broke my Blue Willow plate, smashed my Garrett Snuff glass, and wished me good fortune and God speed. I found employment as a misfit soldier and accumulated GI schooling credits with which I broadened my horizons.

I pursued and outmaneuvered Margaret Gilleland as I was being recalled for active duty in the Korean Police Action. She was but fifteen, while I was an army veteran of twenty, but we got the proper adults to sign papers, and we embarked upon the choppy sea of matrimony in 1950. My bride of better than half a century is a bona fide descendent of the "Old Three Hundred" little Stevie Austin ushered into Texas. She is qualified to sweep the Alamo, or some such nonsense, if she takes the notion.

Aiding and abetting in the creation of this book were Ol' Margaret, my bride of LII years, who did the typing; my compadre, Fred Turner, an unchangeable Yankee computer fanatic; and Brandi Allen, schoolmarm and mother of four young 'uns—Brooklyn, Peyton, Connor, and Jameson. They gave her time off to perform her proofreading expertise.

During my lengthy travel toward dotage, I have accumulated a vast trove of little-known stuff about eerie events and curious capers in our Lone Star State and hereby unleash that avalanche of awe-inspiring data upon an unwary public. What do I expect to get out of it, you might ask?

I don't mind telling you!

Remember back when I presented irrefutable evidence that we're all distant cousins? I'm hoping that you will be moved to buy and treasure this collection of Texas trivia, written by Cousin Charles.

I need the money.

Preface

History writing is an imprecise craft, and compares favorably with the manufacture of high-octane spirits, concocted in the canebrakes and live oak thickets of our land. Practitioners of both trades operate according to secret recipes and use individual ingredients of choice in the final distillation. As validation of that assertion, you should logically grasp the rudiments of each occupation so as to understand fully the striking similarities.

The process of distilling moonshine most likely originated shortly after Adam and Eve got their eviction notice, but the actual date and time is not a part of history, so one can only speculate. The serpent may have been a key player in the beginnings.

A crock container is the first requirement and acts as receptacle for the mash—mash, of course, being the waters, sugars, grain, yeast, and whatever else is on hand. Once the raw materials are hemmed up in that crock, they are stirred vigorously until they abandon their individual identities and become a united conglomeration.

Then the mixture is put into a copper or stainless steel receptacle and heated to a temperature to rival that of a steel mill. A spiral copper umbilical cord is affixed to that seething cauldron, and a catch basin or keg is positioned at the bottom end.

Slowly and surely the finished product will work its way down that copper spiral and arrive in droplets at the chosen container. Voilà, you've got white whiskey! Oftentimes, the nectar is put through the procedure a second time just for kicks, and extra kick is what you get.

The distribution of the finished product can be a chancy maneuver, but there are consumers enough in our land and adjacent lands to keep the art alive—both moonshine and history.

The taste of the differing distilleries' output varies, of course, but that's how you get a horse race. Consumers are usually loyal in their preferences and purchase a particular strain of head cracker, and the secret to success lies in the concocter's hands. This procedure should not be practiced in the confines of your home.

Succinctly, that is how corn is converted from food to drink. Recorded history travels a similar route from the actual event to the printed page, where it is distilled into toddy for your ingestion.

Happenings, dates, and repercussions are collected into a crock receptacle from a multitude of sources and blended with corn, balderdash, and legend by willing and unwilling donors.

These ingredients are infused with yeast and allowed to ferment, for eons in some cases, but distillation can be accelerated to suit the whims of scholars, historians, and the youngster "creeping like snail—unwilling to school" or something like that, according to Will Shakespeare. The history that upsets the stomach least is usually accorded a fermentation period of at least fifty years. Rushed history is often labeled as slanderous and furnishes the stuff from which lawsuits are forged. John Wesley Hardin is a prime example. Following his demise, kinfolk were hard to find, but now the Hardin name is a valued appellation.

The still of history production operates around the calendar, and with admission credentials most anyone can siphon off a batch and alter it to suit himself by the addition of ingredients of personal choice.

I have partaken of the dregs of that historical still and don't mind admitting that I drew understandings and conclusions different from those of most of my betters—but what the hey? This book is composed of Texas history that possibly fell through the cracks and was not included in the selected text you were issued at school. I hope you'll accord charity and lots of room when you judge my efforts.

There exists no rhyme or reason for what has been chosen and what was culled out in the selection process for this presentation of vignettes and episodic accounts of Texana. They are not

arranged in sequential, or for that matter, any discernable, order. The labyrinth configuration is not altogether premeditated but is fashioned to, I hope, command your astonishment, admiration, and adulation. The Greek-alphabet headings of the first and final chapters were affixed for visual impact and the hope of adding additional class.

For clarity's sake, the text is in colored inks. True blue signifies that you are reading plain, unvarnished gospel truth. Red text alerts readers to the possibility of a skirting of actual fact and possibly an outright lie.

The text that is printed in the standard black falls somewhere between those two extremes and you have the prerogative of branding it to suit yourself.

Just recall the feckless crusade of old Diogenes as he stalked the earth with his coal oil lantern. He was seeking an honest man, and if he found one, the incident was omitted from recorded history.

Legend claims that he attended the Universal Convention of History Scriverners back in days gone by, and he reportedly stayed awake during the entire proceedings. He left that august assembly with a disappointed scowl on his face and stalked away in high durgeon, and from that day he was never heard from again.

"There ain't no truth with a capital T!" he lamented as he passed into oblivion.

Thank you for your very kind attention.

The Nth Reader

Daring the Barren Bering

Long before the invention of t-shirts, emblazoned with all manner of slogans and logos, discoverers to be of Texas roamed at will across the vastness between the Rio Grande and the Red River. Flags were the sole method of identifying the home ports for those troublemakers, and there were several of them. Some historians compute that the discovery period began around thirteen thousand years ago, give or take a century. Artifacts and carbonation furnish that evidence, if you've got faith enough in science.

When the Ice Age began to peter out around seven thousand years ago, the Europeans stumbled onto the existence of the North American land mass. In the late 1400s Chris Columbus, in the employ of Ferdinand and Isabella, gave the real estate a cursory examination. He didn't actually see Texas, but he beheld a part of the East Coast and hurried back to Spain with trinkets and samples for the royal court to marvel at.

In 1530, Alvar Nunez Cabeza de Vaca wrecked his ship down near Galveston. He took a wrong turn, and he and a handful of survivors sore footed it west instead of east and wound up in Mexico in 1536. His biggest discovery was how little he enjoyed traipsing through all them Injun camps.

Francisco Vazquez de Coronado was next to step to the plate and do a little exploring and discovering. The Pueblo folk up in the wilds of New Mexico told Frank that the good stuff lay to the east, and he toured the high plains until his spunk waned to mightily near the empty mark.

Whilst Frank Coronado was tromping around in the flatlands up Amarillo way, Hernando De Soto and his expedition were over in the piney woods of East Texas. De Soto died and was relieved by Luis Moscosa de Alvarado, but he too lost interest in the adventure and turned tail in 1542.

Four decades elapsed before much interest in Texas was rekindled, when Fray Agustin Rodriguez struck out up the Rio Grande to do a little preaching. Two other Frays were working the same territory—Juan de Salas and Diego Lopez. They warted the New Mexico tribes until they wore out their welcome and then hastily retreated to the El Paso country. There they stumbled onto Yseleta Pueblo, which is now a part of El Paso and is currently litigating for a gaming permit.

The French provided a diversion with their different colored and decorated pennants in the late 1600s. René Robert Cavelier Sieur de la Salle made his debut in Texas with Mississippi mud on his feet. He'd traced out the mighty Missisip' plumb to where it emptied into the Gulf and claimed French ownership of all the land drained by the Big Muddy.

He hied himself back home, got a few bundles of survey stakes, three more ships, and enough nesters to provide evidence of possession. Alas, he missed the mouth of the Mississippi by about four hundred miles and wound up in Matagorda Bay. Now he'd already lost two ships and his confidence was at low ebb, so he unloaded what stuff and folk he had left and established Fort Saint Louis, just inland from Lavaca Bay.

After he got his countrymen settled in, he gathered his troops and set out by land to see if he could make contact with French outposts spotted along the Mississippi River. He was done in by some of his own troops and planted in Texas in 1687. In Vietnam War jargon, he was "fragged."

The Spanish got their hackles up when they got word of La Salle's incursion, so they dispatched Captain Alonso de Leon to check it out. Fort Saint Louis was in shambles and vacated when he arrived. The French had gotten Indian hackles up too, so they burned the fort, and the survivors fled toward the east.

Father Damian Massanet went along with de Leon, since he enjoyed a frog gig when one presented itself. He struck up a pow wow with Tejas tribal dignitaries, and true to the translation of what they told him, they turned out to be friendly. They invited Father Massanet to conduct a revival since he was already in the area—which he did, and promised to found a permanent mission in the sweet by and by.

He got it done near Weches in Houston County in 1690. Along with religion, he also brought along disease enough to kill off scads of the Tejas natives. Religious fervor fell off dramatically, and Father Massanet felt a calling to go back to Mexico.

The Spanish had tried just about everything to civilize the Indians of Texas, but not much went right for them. Putting the Comanches on horseback ranks high on their boo-boo list, and that set off a domino effect, a shift of rival cultures. The mounted Comanches took Apache land and sent the Jumanos packing to the south, which uprooted the Coahuiltecans and put them in homeless shelters.

Once the French takeover was averted, the Spanish dispatched Fathers Francisco Hidalgo and Antonio Margilda Jesus, who went along with Captain Diego Ramon to study the situation left by the French. They founded several missions over in the piney thickets of East Texas. Their distance from headquarters was a major problem in keeping those religious outposts in operation, so a way station was considered as a solution.

A jumping-off place was erected at San Pedro Springs in 1718. Initially, it was known as San Antonio de Valero, but the profuse growth of cottonwood timber influenced a name change. It became the Alamo, a beehive of business activity and a major livestock center. The large herds of horses and cattle were a source of civic pride, and Apaches were the best customers. They took what they needed as back payment for range lease. They didn't have a flag but still claimed ownership by the adverse possession rule.

"We've been here for seven thousand years," they stated, "and we ain't about to get religion to satisfy a bunch of greedy claim jumpers!" Despite that drawback, the Spanish continued their creation of settlements along the Rio Grande.

Charles III took over Spain in 1759 and appointed Jose

de Galvez to run the show over in New Spain, which was what he called Texas. Jose built a seaport and named it Galveston in the middle to late 1700s and eliminated the long road trips by which goods had always been furnished. He also assumed responsibility for the Louisiana bogs, which had been ceded by the French. He thereby wound up with a boss man in Cuba who was responsible for Louisiana real estate, and a ramrod in Mexico City who operated the Texas, or New Spain, acreage.

Charles IV took over when old III passed on, but he was not near the manager his predecessor had been. His major faux pas was siding with French royalty during the big revolution. When he allied with England to hedge his bet, he spit into the wind.

When Napoleon Bonaparte put himself on top, he had hard feelings toward Charles IV. He got even by selling the whole swampy Louisiana shebang to the United States in 1803. The Anglos began to search for a good place to bridge the mighty Mississippi and Sabine Rivers. The Spanish could see trouble ahead.

Phillip Nolan fudged across the line in the early 1800s, and he was an out-and-out horse thief. His market was east of the Red River. Since he didn't have a lot invested in his horses, he sometimes sold them with a generous rebate and 0 percent financing. His business boomed until he was killed in a battle in the present-day Waco vicinity. His crew was taken into custody and apprenticed out as shovel-and-pick men in the mines of northern Mexico.

Three Spaniards had a simultaneous craving for the oval office and throne. Joseph Bonaparte, a brother to Napoleon, the Bourbon king Charles IV, and Ferdinand VII all coveted the position, and chaos reigned mainly on the plain.

The Cherokee nation was overwhelmed by the influx of immigrants, who were not all that easy to get along with, so, while the top job in Spain was being disputed, the Cherokees packed their belongings and moved into East Texas.

Moses Austin applied for and was awarded the first impresario grant in January 1821. His agreement allowed him to settle three hundred families on the land bordered by the Brazos and Colorado Rivers, the Camino Real on the north, and the Gulf Coast on the south—a sizable chunk of real estate.

Moses died in June of that year, but his son Stephen F. jumped into the breach and led the Old Three Hundred into the Promised Land. Unfortunately for the new colonists, Mexico won its independence from Spain about that time, and negotiations and terms had to be done all over again.

Mexican politics were in turmoil—they had thirty-six presidents between 1833 and 1855—but Austin's deal won sanction and permission to bring in another nine hundred families. He and his new partner, Samuel Adams, were on a roll. By the time 1835 came around, the estimated population of Texas had reached thirty-five thousand, and many of them were openly declaring that independence from Mexico was the only way to go.

Santa Anna, who had taken over the Mexican government, was sorely vexed by what he was hearing. He sent a detachment of crack troops to Anahuac to explain the rules, but William B. Travis headed up a band of revolting settlers and invited the Mexican troops to go west of the Rio Grande. They were not treated graciously, and they did as they were told.

On October 2, 1835, a spirited disagreement arose over custody of a cannon at Gonzales. The six-pound cannon was the property of Mexico, but the Texans would not hear of its being taken away. The first rounds in the Texas Revolution were fired, and some predicted there'd be hell to pay.

Sadly, Colonel Domingo de Ugartechea scrapped his plans for a giant entertainment complex he'd dreamed up and put out for bid. He planned to call it Three Flags Over Texas and locate it in San Antonio. Dreams die hard.

Now, that's the condensed version of what got us from the Bering Strait to San Antonio. If inquiring minds need to know more, there are six thousand versions of this story. The oldest is written in Sanskrit, but this intro is a mandatory drill, and you'll be a better person for having read it. Mercifully, it was done in abstract and in recap brevity.

From here on it'll be easier for you to digest, since it will be in smaller bites. It'll be easier for me, too.

Much Obliged

Thanksgiving Day is observed in the United States annually as a festival of giving thanks for the mercies and blessings of the closing year.

In 1789, the Episcopal Church formally recognized the civil government's authority to anoint such a to-do. In 1888, the Roman Catholic Church decided it was a good idea and bestowed its blessing on the shindig. According to our history, the earliest harvest Thanksgiving celebrated in America was that of the Pilgrim Fathers at Plymouth in 1621.

From 1621 until 1863, the Thanksgiving celebration kind of drifted around, and people got to eating turkey on inappropriate days, but fortunately we got it located and tied down in 1863. The last Thursday in November got the nod, and Thanksgiving Day and Christmas are about the only two we ain't moved to the weekend.

Now, Thanksgiving was not an American invention. Thanksgiving mass was being held all over Europe long before Chris Columbus took a wrong turn. Some of those boat people remembered how much they enjoyed the occasion, and it broke out over here.

And the first recorded Thanksgiving in America was not held in Plymouth!

Captain Francisco Vasquez de Coronado and a bunch of his troops were out in the wide-open spaces avidly seeking gold back in 1541, and the area they were searching was the Panhandle of Texas.

It was spring of the year, and it's too far back to determine whether a blue norther was in operation or whether they encountered a sandstorm, but in either case, it's not hard to imagine how uncomfortable metal underwear could be.

That band of adventurers came across a depression in the landscape that afforded them shelter from the elements, a drink of fresh water, and all the roadrunners they could eat. There and then they manifested their gratitude with all the gusto and fervor they could muster.

The very first Thanksgiving mass in the new world was observed in Palo Duro Canyon on May 23, 1541.

Stuff that information into your turkey and see how much better it tastes.

Traditional Tribulation

A noteworthy New Year's celebration was observed in 1851 at Fort McIntosh, not far from present-day Laredo. The expiring year had been a tad tough due to capricious weather, crop failures, and hair-raising Indian scuffles. The survivors felt like a bona fide night of festivities might be just the ticket to buoy sagging spirits and welcome a new calendar—one they hoped might be a bit more enjoyable.

Like I said, rations were scant, and the menu consisted of black-eyed peas, corndodger, and unlimited spring water.

"I hate black-eyed peas!" old John Blinn snorted, and his discouraging words rang out with gusto. "And, I ain't eatin' any of 'em. You can feed my share to the chickens. I'm going home!"

"We're almighty lucky to have these here peas," Pete Gilleland stated, "and we're fortunate to be free to gather here and salute the coming year."

Alas, John didn't make it home. A party of red men took his horse, his hair, his clothes, and his life within a half-mile of the fort. Bad news can circle the Earth while good news is looking for a sock, and the celebration was quieted when a patrol made the grim report.

"We're lucky to have these black-eyed peas to feast upon and mighty fortunate not to have any prejudices agin' crumbled cornbread and a spring water chaser. It's a tradition we have originated here this day, and the graphic proof is the fate that befell John

Blinn. His tragic demise was a direct result of running smooth out of luck," stated a lay preacher who claimed close ties to the deity.

"He should've et his black-eyed peas," agreed Ernest Gregham. "I'm thankful I stayed for my helping. My hair's way too pretty to wind up on a brave's war lance."

The news spread around Texas, and from that date black-eyed peas were common fare for celebrants and revelers the length and breadth of the Lone Star State. Hope and luck were buoyed upon their ingestion.

The first organized resistance to the tradition reared its ugly head in 1940. College Students at the mess hall of Texas Agricultural and Mechanical College rebelled at what they referred to as "a silly and barbaric superstition."

A cadet who was stuffed with turkey and all the trimmings was appointed spokesperson for the movement. Membership mushroomed, and the ranks swelled like the pain of an impacted tooth.

"The gorging of black-eyed peas on New Year's in the vain desire for good luck is preposterous! We, the collegians of Texas, stand foursquare in opposition to the ridiculous tradition, and we'll not be party to its perpetuation. You can put that in your hat and smoke it!" Don't forget, the spokesman was Clifford Mullet of Texas A & M.

The older and wiser parents and citizens were alarmed and outraged at the audacity of their rebellious sons of academia. With tears in their eyes and fear in their hearts, they beseeched their offspring to reconsider.

"We ain't eatin' no black-eyed peas come New Year's Day," was the response. "So what are you gonna do about it?"

The selection committee for participants in the annual Cotton Bowl Classic responded with alacrity.

"There will be no Southwestern Conference team playing in Dallas on New Year's Day! That's what we're gonna do about it! *No peas, no play!!*" True to their word, teams from outside the conference were invited and quickly accepted.

Clemson pounded Boston College by a six-to-three margin. Those substitute selections were semilogical if you stop and think about it. Bostonians are noted for their love of beans, which a black-eyed pea actually is, and the red-necked South Carolina boys would have downed raw, dried black-eyed peas to make a trip to Big D.

When 1941 rolled around, opposition to black-eyed peas died without a whimper, and as far as I know they have no enemies to this day.

San Saba Silver

Few topics can kindle intense interest more quickly than a legend of a gold or silver mine. Riches that lie waiting to be taken attract the adventurous and the greedy like a magnet affects iron filings. It makes little difference whether the riches are at the bottom of the sea or an excavation into the bowels of the earth.

Fort San Saba was established on the San Saba River back in 1734, and nearby a mission was constructed by Catholic fathers from over Santa Fe way.

The purpose of the fort was to control marauding Comanche Indians, while the avowed function of the mission was Christianizing the red man, but the good work got sidetracked when gold and silver deposits were found in the area. Religious modification was relegated to second place in importance, and it was a distant second.

Three years before Fort San Saba was established, Don Eugenio Domisile had to abandon his mining operation in Peru for financial reasons. His mine was yielding gold enough to make a man rich, but pirates on the high seas had an annoying habit of confiscating his ingots on the way to market.

He and his engineers, miners, and soldiers landed in San Felipe, Mexico, and from there parties were dispatched to search out prospective mining country. One of his men, Martinez Rodrigues, located paydirt near Fort San Saba and found a rich vein of gold. Subsequently, a mule caravan arrived back in San Felipe laden with gold ingots. Another transport train was dispatched immediately but failed to come back. Don Domisile was concerned, of course.

A second party headed for San Saba in the spring of 1735 under the command of Don Antonio Souce. It found the massacred remains of the missing group, and evidence was strong that it'd been done in by Indians. The arrows were still in them.

They continued their journey and located the mines, loaded their mules, and headed back to San Felipe. A day away from San Saba they were attacked, and all but a dozen of the miners were slain—five of them managed to reach the safety of San Felipe and promptly quit their jobs.

While the mining operation had been enjoying limited success, the Christianizing over at the mission was having an extreme case of tough sledding. In 1874 the Indians who were being neglected in the conversion game got so hot and bothered over digging in the mine that they converted all the fathers from living to dead and burned the mission to the ground.

In 1758 another mission was erected, and the Indians were subjected to more brainwashing and baptizing. The mission was destroyed two years later, and there were no survivors, except for the Indians.

The Spanish Crown sent a force of a thousand soldiers and miners to the fort. Mining activities were resumed, and it was business as usual until 1754, when the Indians besieged the fort and leveled it.

The Spaniards, however, didn't give up the ship. They sent Antonio Gomez and a sizable cadre to rebuild the fort and renew the mining operation. Two years later, the Indians destroyed the fort and slew every Spaniard they could catch.

In 1758, Jose de la Amelgamese arrived upon the San Saba scene. Fire was in his eyes, and he brought along two thousand miners and soldiers to bring order and eliminate chaos. With their superior number, the Spanish widened the mining operation, and the gold was carted overland to San Felipe. The silver was also smelted and molded into bars.

The value of silver was considerably lower than that of gold, so the silver ingots were secreted in the mine. The plan was to get the gold to buyers as quickly as possible and later on dig up the silver and take it to market. A year went by, and there was no Indian trouble to cope with. The Spaniards figured they had their bluff in.

However, in 1796 a great religious holiday was observed, and the whole multitude of area Indians was welcomed into the fort for a mass baptizing of Indian children. A battle that registered on the Richter scale ensued, and Spanish blood colored the festival ground. The battle was a decisive victory for the Indians, who forthwith demanded that the Spanish invaders depart the San Saba area and not come back. The alternative was a tomahawk upside their heads, so the Spanish agreed to the plan. While they were loading their equipment, the miners went back into the mines and buried the molded silver bars for pickup at a later time.

The influx of French and English forces made a return inadvisable. The Indians removed all evidence of the mining operation. They even hauled away the accumulated ashes of the smelting fires. The San Saba River was the recipient of all evidence of the entire operation.

When word got around in 1822 about the five separate caches of two thousand bars of silver each, adventurers converged on the area. No evidence was ever found of the filled mines.

Jim Bowie, AWOL from Louisiana, took up with an area tribe in the 1820s, and some claim that he learned the precise locations of the buried silver. Jim left the tribe and went to San Antonio to outfit an expedition to reopen the mine, but he had a run of tough luck and was unable to get back down to San Saba until 1831. When he got there, friends were impossible to find among the Indians. He and his party were set upon in the storied Calf Creek Battle, and Bowie's forces, being hopelessly outnumbered, were forced to retreat and scamper for the safety of San Antonio.

Bowie was not able to assemble another force before he was swept into the turmoil of the revolution mounted against Mexico. Texas independence became his consuming interest. He and an old friend, Moses Rose, joined the Texan forces at the Alamo. Bowie, of course, died at the Alamo. Some claim Rose was the lone male survivor and that he left Texas in shame to live out his life in Louisiana.

If the legend is true, the buried silver is still awaiting discovery.

Moses and Son

Moses parted the waters of the Red River and gained permission to lead three hundred families into Texas in the early 1800s. While it was drying to walking consistency, he went scouting for customers.

Moses Austin was a Connecticut Yankee by birth, but he was a wily negotiator and swung an unheard of deal with the unwary commandant general over in Monterrey. Alas, before the arrangement could be consummated, Moses took to the sickbed and was never able to leave it under his own power. He passed away in 1821.

Stephen Fuller, Moses's son, hated to lose out on the deal his dad had arranged, so he pursued the colonization of Texas with youthful exuberance and vitality. He immediately became the *hefegrande* of the original two hundred immigrants in the first safari. He had intentions of going back for more.

He and his loyal subjects proceeded to an approximate midpoint in the vast territory and established a settlement that is carried unto this day as "Austin" on the official travel map of Texas. "It's," like they say, "a whole other country." The 2002 edition features a suitable-for-framing photograph of governor and Anita Perry and includes the following message:

> Welcome to the great state of Texas. Whether you are a visitor or a resident, I hope you take advantage of the vast and varied opportunities Texas offers.

17

The seven tourism regions of Texas—the Panhandle Plains, Big Bend Country, Hill Country, Prairies and Lakes, Piney Woods, South Texas Plains, and the Gulf Coast—abound with diverse environmental settings for business and personal enjoyment. Enjoy your travels along the more than 79,000 miles of excellent Texas highways and byways; and whatever your purpose or destination, drive safely and help keep Texas beautiful. (Signed) Rick Perry, Governor of Texas

You might note when you study your personal copy of the official travel map that Governor Perry prints his autograph and uses uppercase letters throughout—with the exception of E and Y. They are lowercase and may very well be the approved teaching at Paint Creek Texas.

Another famous Texan also has a bit of advice, but unfortunately it is not included in the official travel map. "Don't mess with Texas," is what Willie Nelson always says, and he sometimes adds, "Be sure and put your snipes in the ashtray—but empty that ashtray ever chance you get!"

We've strayed from our original topic, and it is high time we finished the saga of Stephen Fuller Austin. He was born in Wythe County, Virginia, in 1792, was still a Virginian when his father passed away, and it was he who guided the first bunch of American colonists to the Texas state of Mexico.

The settlers were a gritty bunch, and they managed to make a go of it. Apparently others got the good news, and they began to pour into Texas in prodigious numbers. By 1833, they were sufficiently numerous to hold a convention with the aim of drawing up a constitution for statehood. They neglected to inform the Mexican government of their intentions, but once the meeting ended, they decided they should send a delegation down to Mexico City and see if they could get it ratified. Stephen Austin was one of the delegates, who made a few stabs at making their presentation to the proper authorities, but without any luck.

Revolution, unrest, and chaos were rampant south of the border, and in desperation Austin mailed a letter to the head honcho and advised him of the planned formation of a state under the active constitution of May 7, 1824. Austin was promptly arrested for treasonable behavior, jugged, and held hostage pending proper behavior by the wild-eyed Texan colonists.

Stephen cooled his heels for a couple of years in a Mexican hoosegow and rued his sins. In September of 1835, he certified his loyalty to Mexico and in November was appointed as a commissioner to the United States.

At a stopover in New Orleans, Stephen learned that Santa Anna had joined with the Federalists and that the invasion of Texas was the first matter on their agenda. He scurried back to Austin and, with Sam Houston, rallied the Texan wannabees into an army for independence. Of course, everyone knows how that turned out.

Stephen lost his presidential bid for the Republic of Texas throne to his old crony Sam Houston, who appointed Austin as secretary of state. Stephen died two days after Christmas Day in 1836, but he will always be remembered as the father of Texas and the son of Moses.

Fredonia Misfire

The colonization of Texas by American settlers got off to a good start when Stephen Austin led the first two hundred families into the central part of the state. The Mexican government dealt out liberal grants of land for distribution to the newcomers, and the emigrants reciprocated with model behavior and conversion to the Catholic Church.

In 1826, Haden Edwards was granted permission to settle eight hundred families, and he opted to make his settlement at Nacogdoches, over on the east side of Texas, within walking distance of the Sabine River.

Already residing in the area were a goodly number of Spanish-speaking citizens who had been on the land for several years, but they did not have legal title to their acreage. There were a few American wetbacks who had sneaked into Texas and were in the same boat as their Spanish neighbors. Since there was land aplenty for everyone, Haden did not disturb those people, who were plainly squatters.

Haden had yet another neighbor to whom he extended his hand in friendship. A sizable tribe of Cherokee Indians also called Nacogdoches home. Haden Edwards then suffered a severe case of bad judgment. He took sides with the Cherokees and decided that the Spanish could vamoose and go back to Mexico.

He declared Texas independent of Mexico and changed the official state name to Fredonia. He split his take into two equal

21

parcels and told the Cherokees that half belonged to them. Haden then invited the Americans in other colonies to side with him and take all of Texas from Mexico.

The response he received was not at all what he expected. A force of Mexican military showed up and explained things to Haden in terms a child could grasp. Along with the Mexicans were a number of members from Austin's colony, and their opinion of the way things should be handled matched that of the Mexican government.

Not a single shot was fired, and there were no fatalities in the Fredonian War of 1826. Howsomever, 1836 was but a decade distant, and business began to pick up.

Sam Served

Sam Houston made a lot of tracks in his seventy-year visit to this planet. He was born around Lexington, Virginia, on the second day of March 1793. As a lad of thirteen he was left fatherless, and his family relocated to the wilds of Tennessee, where Sam came down with rambling fever.

He left home, crossed the Tennessee River, took up with the Indians, and adapted to their way of living. Oolooteka, a chief, took such a shine to Sam that he adopted him as a son.

Sam meandered back to his original home in 1811, and when he couldn't find steady work, he up and founded a school. He taught readin', writin', and cipherin', with a shop class in arrowhead manufacturing and archery, but he was not satisfied with that life either.

The military life beckoned, and in 1813 Sam joined the U.S. Army, and there he found his niche. He advanced in rank to ensign, then to lieutenant, and attracted the eye of General Andy Jackson, along with his friendship and admiration.

In the battle of Tallapoosa, Sam sustained an injury that robbed him of certain of his appurtenances and sorely hindered the usefulness of what he had left. Sam didn't whimper over the matter, but his future plans were affected by his loss. But like they say, "life goes on." Sam took up with the bottle and developed a drinking problem. The problem was in drinking enough.

In 1817, Sam was back in operation and was appointed to the

post of Indian subagent to see that treaty terms with the Cherokees were adhered to, to the letter.

"I'm the man for the job," he stated with due humility. "I speak their language." In the course of business, he escorted a delegation of Indians to Washington and was stunned by the reception he received. Complaints abounded about his behavior in resisting the unlawful importation of African slaves into Florida, since Florida was a Spanish province.

Sam was acquitted of all charges, but his feelings were badly bruised, and he resigned his commission in the army, returned to Tennessee, and took up the study of law in Nashville. His education yielded instant success. In 1819, he was elected district attorney and in 1821 was anointed major general of the militia.

Two years later, he was elected to Congress and was reelected in 1825. In 1827, he was named governor of Tennessee.

In January 1829, Miss Eliza Allen consented to be his wife. She was in the upper crust of Tennessee society, and Sam was a proud man once the "I do's" were said. The marriage lasted three months. Eliza packed her duds and left the premises in a huff. No reasons were forthcoming, but speculation around Tennessee was that Sam had not presented all the proper credentials.

Sam resigned his office and struck out for Arkansas and his Indian friends. He hung around with that bunch for three years, until his feet got itchy at the outbreak of the Mexican War. He was elected commander in chief of the Texas army before he had time to water his horse. Sam held that job until Texas won its independence in 1836.

In July, a general election to seat a president, a vice president, and a congress was slated for the first Monday in September. Sam was encouraged to run for the top position, but at first he nixed the thought and enjoyed the tranquility of life on the sidelines. The pressure to seek the presidency increased, and finally Sam agreed to put his hat in the ring. He started late in the game with only eleven days to campaign, but he whipped Stephen F. Austin, Henry Smith, and T. J. Green by a vote tally of 3,585 to a total of 737 split up among the three also-rans.

Sam was inaugurated on October 22, 1836. His first act as president was the release of Santa Anna, who'd been kept in a cage since being blindsided by the Texas army at San Jacinto. Sam had been in command of the winners.

Then he began negotiating with the U.S. government for statehood. President Jackson said he had problems enough without admitting Texas to the Union. Texas was completely without funds or prospects of having any.

Sam married Margaret Moffietta Lea of Alabama in 1840, and she accepted him with all his flaws. She got him off the booze, and he joined the Baptist Church.

Sam was reelected in 1841 and pulled another hitch as president, but his pleas for statehood were refused with disdain.

Finally, in 1845, Texas was admitted to the Union, and Sam was one of the first senators from Texas to cross the Mississippi on official business. In recognition of his good works, he was reelected to the Senate in 1853. He held that post until March 1859, when he came home to Texas and became governor. His opposition to Texas's seceding from the Union led to his being removed from that eminence. "I worked too hard to get Texas into the Union to allow us to throw in the towel and call it quits," he stated. He retired to Huntsville and abstained from politics and alcoholic beverages until his death.

Houston, the city, is named for him, and there's a county with the Houston tag on it over in East Texas.

First Fall of the Alamo

Mexican Army Beaten and Ousted from San Antonio and Alamo Mission" was the headline on December 11, 1835. "After five days of constant combat, and the loss of 150 soldiers, General Martin Cos raised the flag of surrender. Texian losses were reported as 28. Cos was allowed to gather his troops and return to the Mexico that lies west of Rio Bravo Del Norte. Cos, speaking for the Mexican Government, vowed with his word of honor that all conflict was ended for evermore."

The trouble began when Santa Anna became *el Presidente* of all Mexico in 1833, and his secret agenda was to "put those gringo Texians in their place."

He sent General Martin Cos, who was also his brother-in-law, to patrol the border and enforce immigration laws. Santa Anna had a sneaking feeling that those Texians had a plot ready for hatching, and the thought was revolting. He told General Cos to scare the daylights out of those pushy immigrants.

Thirty thousand Texas colonists were aided and abetted by fierce Comanches and other Indians who had a dislike for Mexican tyranny. Three hundred volunteers arrived from Georgia, and two companies of Louisiana sympathizers hurried over from New Orleans, bringing munitions and supplies.

Cos dispatched Colonel Ugartechia to Gonzalez with orders to pick up a brass cannon that was Mexican property. The Texians allowed Ugartechia's troops to look down the barrel and then fired

a cannon ball. The Mexicans only lost one man, but they went home without the cannon. That scuffle took place on October 2, 1835, and the report of that six-pounder reverberated at Mexico City.

Ben Milam, Edward Burleson, Deaf Smith, and Jim Bowie, along with their men, rode south for a piece of the action. David Crockett came from Tennessee, with old "Betsy" primed and ready for battle. The entire volunteer army converged in the San Antonio area.

Ben Milam planned and headed up a night attack on Goliad's garrison. Routed from sleep, the garrison surrendered, and twenty-five soldiers, along with the commander, surrendered. A sizable cache of rifles, some artillery pieces, and ten thousand dollars in cash and supplies were the victors' spoils. The Texians took Goliad without any loss of life.

Bowie and Fannin with a ninety-man force marched on San Antonio, which was headquarters for the four hundred troops under the command of General Cos.

The first contact occurred on October 27. In a half-hour melee, a hundred Mexican soldiers were killed, and the Texans took custody of yet another cannon. At that time, the Texian main force had not arrived, but it was not far behind. The siege of San Antonio began.

For five days at close-quarters, pitched battles raged from street to street and house to house. By the time General Cos raised the white flag, 150 of his soldiers lay dead or dying. The Texas forces lost twenty-eight, and old Ben Milam was one of that number.

The Texians set up their headquarters in a deserted mission called the Alamo. The victors extracted an agreement, on his word of honor, from General Cos. He vowed that neither he and his men nor any other Mexican force would ever again mess with the Texas army. General Cos limped home and made a full report to his brother-in-law, Santa Anna.

Santa Anna felt no obligation to honor the sacred promise Cos had made. Brothers-in-law are like that sometimes.

The Price of Independence

The call went out, and fifty-nine men braved the cold north wind and traveled to Washington on the Brazos, the pro tem capital of the embryonic Republic of Texas. The called meeting was scheduled to draw up a declaration of independence from Mexico, and they meant to sign it on March 2, 1836, as a birthday gift for Sam Houston, a Tennessean who was often referred to as the Big Daddy of Texas. Sam was turning forty-two that day, and he was "swole up" like a toad frog just thinking about his expected gift.

There'd been considerable differences in opinion betwixt the town fathers of San Felipe de Austin and Washington on the Brazos as to which city would host the historic to-do.

Back in 1835, delegates had bunched up at San Felipe to bare gripes about tacky treatment by the Mexican government, and many of the attendees had been disgruntled about accommodations. Businessmen and merchants down Washington way were more adept tub-thumpers, however, so San Felipe came in second.

Noah Byars owned the biggest building in Washington. Noah was a blacksmith by trade, but he was also a fair-to-middling hustler. He had been as busy as a beaver forging firearms for the expected war against Mexico.

A Mr. Boatright and Sam Gilleland approached Mr. Byars immediately after San Felipe won the nod of the delegation. They owned a goodly acreage of prime development property in the area, and they were not rank amateurs at hustling either.

"There's going to be a lot of folks coming to town on the first of March, Noah," Boatright said.

"Do tell," Noah responded. "Do you reckon they need to buy some guns?"

"Hard to say," Sam said, "but what they're up to might make your business boom. They plan on drawing up papers to run the Mexicans plumb out of Texas!"

"Good idea," Noah agreed, "but how does that affect me now? I got a heap more guns than I know what to do with already."

"They need a sizable building to meet in," Sam said. "You've got the biggest one in town and we'd like to have them get together in here. We're authorized to offer you 170 dollars to rent your place for three days."

Noah operated his bellows fiercely as he studied over the proposition. Most likely his mind was already made up, but he didn't want to appear easy or eager. He'd been planning the enlargement of his building for some time, and the lack of cash had stood in the way of expansion. He, of course, agreed, and Noah, Boatright, and Gilleland shook hands on the deal. They promised payment after the delegation completed their meeting.

Alas, one thing led to another, and Noah did not completely manage the intended enlargement project. He got the walls up and a roof over it, but there was no glass in the windows, and the doors were not hung.

The north wind moaned like a banshee, and the temperature hovered around the thirty mark. They hung tarps over the gaping windows and doors, but even with the forge warmed to the melting point it was still almighty chilly. Nary a coat was removed, and those without gloves sat on their hands. It was not a happy time for the fifty-nine assembled souls.

"We'll all die of pneumonia if this meeting lasts over three days and the wind don't lay," Bill Gregory said.

George Childress, who had published the *Nashville Banner* back in Tennessee, was nominated, accepted, and acted as chairman of the committee to prepare the declaration of independence. Some said that he had the declaration when he arrived at the meeting, and if that is true it was an act of mercy. The north wind raged unabated, and within an hour George Childress stood before the assembly and read the rough draft. It sounded a lot like the American Declaration of Independence, but not a single complaint was heard. It was approved without debate, and every man in the group was anxious to sign and leave for home.

But it was not to be. Those gentlemen took off from their labors and spent the entire day of March 2 celebrating old Sam Houston's forty-second birthday. The north wind even abated a tad to commemorate that historic occasion.

They reconvened on March 3, headaches and all, and affixed their names to the corrected document. Noah Byars offered to sign, since he was furnishing the meeting hall. He wandered among the delegates at their break times and did his dead-level best to peddle a few of his guns. Noah struck out on both pursuits. He was reminded that he was a compensated caterer and that salesmen were prohibited by law from hawking their wares at a formal gathering of the delegation. He sulked a bit at the rebuff and allowed the warmth from his forge to wane accordingly.

The document was duly and officially executed on March 3, and a hundred copies were produced so that delegates might have evidence for show and tell when they arrived back at their home and hearth. The March 2 date on the declaration was inaccurate, but nobody seemed to care.

Childress and a friend took responsibility for putting a certified copy in the hands of the proper authorities. Some contend that the historic document from Washington, Texas, never made it to Washington, D.C. Mr. Kemble, a delegate from the wilds of Kentucky, cabbaged onto the treasured paper and got off with it. Investigation of the debacle later proved that the signed declaration was indeed delivered to Washington, D.C., but that it was misplaced while the bureaucracy was deliberating on a Texas request for some financial aid for the noble cause. Which was turned down.

It turns out that a minister Sam Houston sent up to D.C. to represent Texas had given the document to a trusted friend in that high place. Naturally it was mislaid, and neither hide nor hair of it was discovered until 1896.

Handling was expedited once it was located, and it was

returned to authorities at Austin in 1929. If you crave to see it, it is on display in a hallowed niche on the first floor of the capitol.

Only two of the signers of the Texas Declaration of Independence were natural, native-born Texans, and both of those gentlemen were Señors. They were Jose Antonio Navarro and Jose Francisco Ruiz. Ruiz attended the convention, with a definite handicap, since he did not speak or understand much English, but he seated himself near an interpreter and did his duty.

Tennessee and Virginia provided eleven signers each, North Carolina furnished nine, Kentucky kicked in five, while Georgia and South Carolina anted up four each. The Yankee tribes provided as best they were able: Pennsylvania furnished four, New York two, and Massachusetts managed a single entry, the same as the old South's Mississippi, which provided a single delegate. In addition, the quorum was reached by a single signer from England, Ireland, Canada, and Mexico, respectively.

In case you're wondering how Noah P. Byars came out, you may not be surprised to learn that he was never paid for the use of his blacksmith shop. Messrs. Boatright and Gilleland blamed Noah for the loss of the capital site to the city of Austin. They claimed that the delegation voted fifty to one against doing any further business with Washington on the Brazos—winter or summer.

Sam's Birthday 1836

Sam Houston turned forty-two on March 2, 1836, and the bunch he was running with went out of their way to present him with a gift he'd coveted for a good while. It had been manufactured the previous day at Washington on the Brazos.

"Happy birthdays" were administered with high good spirit, and Sam got his copy of a document declaring Texas's independence from Mexico.

"Declaring independence is one thing," Sam smiled gratefully, "but making it stick may cause a ruckus! General Santa Anna is down at San Antonio right now, and he brought a lot of his friends with him. Some will tell you that he ain't too happy. We're gonna need an army with a strong leadership to get any respect from the Mexican government!"

Two days later, Sam Houston was elected to lead the Texas revolutionary army, and he started out in the hole. Texas forces at the Alamo fell under prolonged siege and were defeated on March 6. Texans were faint-hearted and fearful, and some questioned the wisdom of the brash actions being taken by the firebrands in their midst.

"Texas has made a bad mistake!" was a common observation. "Santa Anna's gonna whup us and send the survivors back east of the Mississippi, as sure as skunks smell!" History has shown, of course, that the doomsayers were wrong. General Sam surprised

the world and Santa Anna at San Jacinto on April 21, 1836, and gave his army a sound drubbing.

The dust of battle had scarcely settled before folks began to talk about applying for statehood in the United States of America. That ambition was slow in bearing fruit. Statehood was realized on December 29, 1845.

In the meantime, Texas bore its independence with a lot of style and little money.

Our first president was named Gouverneur. David Gouverneur Burnett to be precise, and eight months of the presidency was all he could stand.

"You ramrodded this deal," he told Sam Houston, "so you can run it!"

Sam could—and did. He served as our second president and as our fourth. He even pulled a hitch as governor after Texas was granted statehood. He governed the state from 1859 to 1861.

"I was a governor long before I came to Texas," he's reported as saying, "and after being a president, this governor business is too small potatoes for me to mess around with!'

It's fortunate for us all that our declaration of independence was given to Sam Houston as a birthday gift.

There'd been talk of independence for a long time, and we almost made our declaration two days before old Sam's birthday.

Had that occurred, Texas would now be in its forty-first year; 1836 was a leap year!

Super Brawl

Skilled, and preferably sober, surveyors were as rare on the North American continent as unicorns when need for a fifty-yard line arose. And to complicate the game, the playing field was not precisely level, but since a cue ball looks flat to a germ, never was heard a disparaging word. That makeshift fifty-yard line is shown on maps of today and is popularly know as the Rio Grande.

At the beginning of the "big game," the Mexican All-Stars pretty much held sway over the whole shebang of land straddling the Rio Bravo Del Norte. There were a continuous series of scrimmages to report, but the lack of even a primitive newsletter caused the incursions, penetrations, and other stats to go mostly unreported.

Moses Austin, in a roundabout way, threw down the gauntlet when he was permitted the importation of a ragtag team from the East, which he dubbed the Texians. His first batch was billed as the Old Two Hundred, but alas, Moses took sick and was rendered unable to manage the team. His favorite son, Stephen, seized the moment and assumed leadership when his old papa gave up the ghost.

Almost immediately, preparations for the Super Brawl began, and the native residents began their scalping operations, as a diversionary attraction.

Not only that, the opposing teams were continually in turmoil, and rule changes sorely vexed the Texian team, so they straw-voted Stephen Austin to the quarterback post. He named Sam Houston as his offensive assistant, and tailgate parties became commonplace amongst the Texian squad. Taunts were bandied to and fro between the two teams, and fistfights were not uncommon.

The Texians were sore about the ownership and management of the playing field, and the bolder ones threatened to take the eastern half of the field by negotiation if it could be done with alacrity. That failing, they offered to play for the title, with no holds barred.

The Mexican All-Stars were not all that keen on laying on the line the title to the real estate unless the Texians had something of value to put in the pot.

"How about Louisiana and Alabama?" Sam Houston asked slyly. "We lose, I'll sign a quit claim deed!"

"Done!" said the Mexican quarterback. "Who takes the kickoff?"

"We'll flip for it," Sam stated.

"I'll do the flipping," Santa Anna agreed, and he did it forthwith. When the peso descended to his palm, he studied it momentarily and announced, "We win the toss!"

"We've got to keep a wary eye upon them suckers," Sam told Steve. "They'll bear watching mighty close!"

"So will we, Sam. So will we." Stephen smiled in anticipation. "Let the game begin!" he bellowed, and the jug band swung into a spirited rendition of "I've Been Working on the Railroad."

The mariachi band of the opponents performed "Deguallo" with brass accompaniment. The literal meaning of the tune was lost on Sam and Stephen, but they were not concerned.

"We didn't come here to lose," they muttered and went about girding their loins.

Santa Anna, or as teammates referred to him, Tony, mounted a formidable offense. He charged across the fifty and ate up yardage at a terrible pace until he ran into the vaunted Alamo defense of the Texians. From that point, the innocent game became a veritable war.

"Them suckers has got us outnumbered, Stephen," Sam stated. "We'd best turn the quarterbacking over to a guy who just arrived from the wilds of Tennessee. Name's Travis, but he's got a lot of grit in his craw and they ain't no quit in him. You and me will be worth more to the team if we get the heck out of here and scout out a few substitutes. It blamed sure looks like we're gonna need 'em." They lit a shuck at the first commercial break and high-tailed it to the rear.

Well sir, historical records abound on the way that initial defense dug in and defended their turf to the last man, but the superior number of Mexicans scored six, tried for two, and made that also. The score early in the first quarter was in favor of the Mexicans by an eight-to-zip edge. Stephen and Sam fretted, of course, and redoubled their scouting for more frontline cannon fodder, but they did it well away from the playing field.

A farm team was called in as replacements for the Texians. Jim Fannin was the signal caller down Goliad way. He was West Point trained and stiff-necked to a fault. He paid little heed to Sam's suggestion that he play possum and stall for time until the Mexican team began to tire. The Goliad defense failed.

Another wipeout, and an additional six points. Luckily the extra-point try failed due to an offsides penalty, but the score ballooned to thirteen-zip. Tony's team did high fives and cavorted in exultation, as the first half ended.

"Man, this is too easy," gloated Tony. "I'm calling an additional time out, and we'll mosey on down to a place I know where the living is easy and take us a siesta, following a succulent repast and liquid of three-worm excellence. You amigos will love San Jacinto!" Which they did.

At half-time, the Texians looked at their hole card and it turned out that Sam Houston's likeness was on it. He was nominated and elevated to QB status of the bedraggled cast of misfits and broken-spirited players. They had all the earmarkings of a squad that might just roll over and give up. Sam delivered an oration to reinspire and rekindle the flames from the barely glowing embers beneath the ashes of defeat.

"Let me tell you something, men," he roared. "Them Mexicans is drunk with power and flush with easy scores—but we're gonna make a comeback of historic proportions! We're going to blindside them like they ain't never been blindsided down at San Jacinto! The power is with us! I have had me a vision that tells of our victory. San Jacinto is an acronym that foretells our good fortune in the next series."

"Yeah, yeah," they responded. "You're feeding us baloney, balderdash, and poppycock. Besides, we don't know what in tarnation an acronym is," someone added.

Patiently Sam explained acronyms to a mostly uninterested crowd, and once they grasped the drift of it, Sam paused dramatically, raised one finger heavenward, and roared. "Santa Anna Napped. Just About Croaked In Nervy Texian Onslaught! That was the gist of my revelation boys, and I've never knowed an acronym to fail. The Mexicans is as good as whupped. Mark my words, load your rifles, and follow me. We're about to make the comeback of all time!'

Sam's prophecy came to pass, but they did not rely on the finesse of the forward pass atall. They resorted to down-and-dirty ground play, right through the line. Within twenty minutes, the Mexicans who were still mobile were beneath tubs, and the waving of white flags resembled a Klan rally. The Texians went for two and scored handily.

Score: All-Stars 14, Texians 8.

Total confusion reigned among the Mexicans, and they fumbled the ensuing kickoff on their own goal line when they were unable to locate their quarterback. Tony had left the field of play for the safety of the tall timber, but Sam assured his team that since Tony was afoot he'd be back. "He runs in circles since he lost that foot in the battle of Tampico," Sam said. Tony had vamoosed like a good intention, and the Texians fell heir to a quick two via the "safety rout."

Score: Los Amigos 14, Texians 10.

Time was called, and Tony was finally shackled and ushered to the concession stand area. He was determined to be unfit for additional play and withdrew from the game. The game was into the early moments of the fourth quarter and had become an uninteresting defensive battle. It was learned that the Texians were considering jumping to another league, the U.S. Stars, and business picked up again.

League president Polk sent Zach Taylor down from the far East to strengthen the Texians. Quarterback Zach was aided by yet another import. Winfield Scott completed the rout deep in enemy territory, and the Texians were awarded all the real estate east of the fifty-yard line and considerable acreage up north, mighty near reaching the south line of Canada. It was an easy touchdown, but the extra-point try failed when Zach made his famous remark about what he'd do if he owned Hell and Texas. He, of course, claimed he'd live in Hell and rent out Texas.

Final Score: Los Amigos 14, Texians 16.

The Texians then joined the Red Neck Rebels but lost their first game fair and square to the Yankee Bunch in a bitterly contested game, which was publicized by Margaret Mitchell in her romantic account of Rhett and Scarlett's flaming affair.

Now, the losers in the Super Brawl fell into the practice of siestas, but they didn't forgive and forget their loss to the Texians. They did not sleep all the time, and as the 1900s ran their course and yielded to a new century, Mexicans fell heir to a brand new GM. He is regarded as a sly fox, and oddly enough, that is his actual name. Vincente Fox to be precise. He is sophisticated, highly intelligent, and he has beguiled his U.S. counterpart into a rematch, which is now under way. Future generations will refer to the titanic struggle as Super Brawl II.

East of the Rio Grande, the opposition is regarded as Bush League by Fox, since that GM is not even unilingual. There was no designated "no man's land" in this match. The fifty-yard line is crossed in both directions, at will, by Mexicans or Bush Leaguers, and the coaching of the Texians was in contention with a possible Mexican sympathizer going up against Slick Rick from Paint Creek, who was left in charge when George lit a shuck for the big time over in Washington on the Delaware.

Tony Sanchez threw down the gauntlet and had money, motivation, and moxie enough to give Rick a run for his money. He was a bona fide Texan, but check out the way his name is spelled. Tony lost, of course.

And, bear in mind, Tony was a generous contributor to George's "going east" fund.

The last such GM (Governor Monarch) with a Spanish surname was Ramon Eca y Musquiz, back in 1835. He was running the Texas show when Sam and Stephen formed the Texian team.

It was a great game.

The Yellow Rose

Nope, that ain't a song title in this context. With due apologies to Bob Wills, of Turkey, Texas, I hereby submit a tale, based on historical fact, of a little-known incident that occurred at the site of the Alamo in 1836, near the dawning of the Republic of Texas.

Until Colonel William B. Travis drew his legendary line in the sand and asked those who were willing to die for Texas independence to step across, he commanded a patchwork army of 183 men. They all stepped across—except for one. That one was known as Moses.

Louis "Moses" Rose wound up at the Alamo by a circuitous route that is staggering to the imagination. He was born in France in 1785 and joined Napoleon's army while still in his teens. He served as well as any man until the French campaign was stymied by bitter cold and stiff Russian resistance in 1812, when the siege of Moscow failed. Thousands of Napoleon's soldiers died in that failed assault, but Moses was a survivor and managed to get back to France in one piece. His loyalty was unfaltering even after Napoleon was beaten and exiled. Moses participated in a plot to restore Napoleon to power, but when the plan failed the entire group was expelled from France—forevermore. The alternative to disobeying was death. Moses emigrated to the United States and found his way to Louisiana.

Texas was still a part of Mexico, but many Americans were relocating there as settlers. As that number increased, the settlers

began to speak bluntly of a desire for independence, but the Mexican army held sway through might, and talk of rebellion became whispers instead of demands.

Hayden Edwards changed that in 1826, when he commanded an armed force and wrested Nacogdoches from the iron grasp of Mexico. Moses Rose was one of his soldiers.

The Mexican army returned and easily dominated the brash upstart Texans.

Colonel James Bowie assembled yet another army, retook

Nacogdoches, and ran the Mexican garrison out of the area. Bowie's handpicked force of twenty included Moses Rose. Those twenty men conquered and routed the entire force of better than three hundred trained Mexican soldiers.

Bowie applauded the bravery of Moses Rose, and the two became close friends. A sawmill owner, John Durst, deeded Moses Rose a hundred-acre farm in appreciation for his actions in the coup. Moses was grateful, of course, and announced his plan to settle down and become a farmer.

In 1835, however, a full-scale war against Mexican rule loomed, so Moses sold his farm, joined his friend Jim Bowie, and went to San Antonio. Once there, both fought alongside General Edward Burleson's forces and helped take San Antonio from the Mexican army.

Bowie was given command of the Texas force and promptly relocated his men to a small mission on the fringe of San Antonio. That mission was the Alamo.

General Santa Anna took a very dim view of the actions of the upstart Texans and immediately activated an army of five thousand to dislodge and eradicate the Texans at the Alamo.

For ten days, the superior number of Mexican troops subjected the force of 182 rebels to continuous bombardment and assault and the strains of "Deguallo." Thus began the battle that will be remembered and discussed until time is no more. At show-and-tell time, the defenders of the Alamo were challenged to step across the line if they would pledge their lives for Texas independence. The final outcome was inevitable. Moses Rose was the only man who did not cross the saber line drawn in the sand.

In the dark of night on March 3, he climbed over the bullet-scarred wall of the Alamo and picked his way through the dead bodies and found an escape route.

He walked to Iola, a small settlement in Grimes County and went to the home of an old friend. Abraham Zuber was surprised to see Moses alive. The March 24 *Telegraph and Texas Register* had reported him as one of the Alamo casualties.

Moses told his story to Mr. Zuber, and in 1873 William Zuber, Abraham's son, wrote an article, "An Escape from the Alamo," which was published in the *Texas Almanac*.

Moses returned to his hometown of Nacogdoches but found no friendship or forgiveness for his being alive. He stayed there until 1842, but was shunned and avoided. He was unable to regain any degree of acceptance.

Finally, Moses left Texas in 1842 and made his way to Logans Port in De Soto Parish, Louisiana, and remained there until his death in 1850.

There is information that he was buried in Ferguson Cemetery, located on Castoff Creek, which was reportedly named to dishonor the memory of Louis Moses Rose.

Some students of history claim that he was actually buried near Mount Pleasant, Texas, but no one knows for sure.

The warrior who battled bravely on a battlefield in Russia, a trusted and dependable crusader beside James Bowie, will only be recalled for the one time he was too weary of conflict to stand his ground.

Louis Moses Rose will be remembered only as the Yellow Rose of Texas.

Neuces Nuisance

The strip of land lying between the Nueces and Rio Grande was, and still is, a formidable expanse of real estate. When Santa Anna, under considerable duress, conveyed Texas to Sam Houston in 1836, they agreed that the land lying east of the Rio Grande belonged to the Republic of Texas, but there were a few who did not concur with Santa Anna's conveyance.

Take, for instance, the father of Trinidad Cortina. He obtained a land grant from the king of Spain and settled in Texas in 1767. His son became heir to the place, and Juan caused quite a ruckus in July 1859. Texas had evolved into a bona fide state of the United States at that time, but young Juan Cortina was not awed by that fact. And he proved it by word and by deed.

Juan was born west of the Rio Grande—but not far to the west. Trinidad had died when Juan was a baby, and his mother relocated her brood of children across the river and onto Texas soil. Not wanting for money, she built a showplace home, the Rancho Santa Rita, a few miles upriver from Brownsville. She reared her children to be gentle but made the mistake of hiring a less than honest manager for the Santa Rita. He turned out to be a land-grabbing, thieving crook of great ability at separating un-hip landowners from their real estate by legal maneuvers that would stand up in court. In his favor.

Little Juan watched as his mother and several neighbors were robbed of their land. The Indian fierceness of his father began to fester in Juan at these outrages, and as he neared manhood, he decided that it was high time he got into the game.

The Strip, lying between the Neuces and the Rio Grande, became a hotbed for shysters and swindlers in the real estate profession, and Charles Stillman, a native of the New England tribes, rose to the position of top man in the trade. He had established himself in South Texas by selling guns and ammunition to Mexican rebels across the Rio Grande, and then he branched out and dabbled in real estate, acquired by the time-proven method of title by trickery.

Many acres of Cortina land had accrued unto Stillman by this method, and along with the land he gained custody of the salt lakes to the north. The lakes had been a particular treasure of the Cortinas and a dependable source of income from salt addicts of the area.

Another recognition of Stillman's extraordinary abilities was his elevation to the unofficial post of political heavyweight champion of Brownsville. He ruled and managed the semiannual grand jury and had a hand in the selection of those deserving of indictments.

These accomplishments also earned Stillman the intense hatred of young Juan Cortina. Juan was indicted on murder charges at each and every grand jury session, but those warrants were seldom served.

Juan, realizing that he was a marked man, began to recruit other disgruntled young men to oppose the exploiters of the Mexican landowners in the strip, who were almost helpless against the land-grabbing tactics of the Stillman faction.

Soon, the citizens of Brownsville realized that they were about to have a big problem with the Cortinistos, since their number was increasing at an alarming rate. A town meeting was called to hire a town marshal to oppose the Cortina faction. The money was appropriated, and Bob Shears was put on the payroll as sheriff of Brownsville.

His first assignment was to arrest and bring Juan Cortina to trial. Stillman's hand-selected judges were standing by to put Juan and his band of men behind bars. Sheriff Shears bunched all the accumulated indictments into a small bale and bided his time, waiting for Juan Cortina to show his face in Brownsville. His wait was rewarded on July 13, 1859. Juan and four other men rode in and entered a saloon just off Market Plaza, while the sheriff watched with great interest. The fourth rider crossed the street and entered a café. He apparently had more of an appetite for food than a thirst for drink.

Stillman sent word for his deputies to report for duty, but while he waited he made the decision to go into the café and make an arrest by himself. Bad decision!

The diner, Pedro Juarado, saw him approaching and ran out the door, bent on joining his amigos at the saloon. Stillman shoved his six-shooter into Pedro's middle and commanded him to get back into the café.

Juan, with one foot on the rail, saw what was happening, walked outside, and mounted his horse. In a heartbeat, he was across the street and charging through the café's open front door, just as Sheriff Shears was relieving Pedro of his firearm. Juan fired, and Shears, badly wounded, hit the floor. The other customers lost their appetites at that arresting spectacle and vamoosed out the back door.

The summoned deputies were nearing the area when Juan emerged on his mount with an arm around Pedro's waist and dashed across the street. As Pedro and the other three mounted their horses, Juan sprayed the deputy force with lead. They ran for cover as Juan and his men galloped out of town, shooting and yelling like Comanches. As a final insult, Juan put a single shot through a plate glass window of Stillman's Real Estate. The war had commenced with a bang, courtesy of Juan Cortina's first show of defiance.

The citizenry of Brownsville were spooked by the incident. Fear of losing their lives was thick enough to cut with a knife—especially amongst the real estate dealers.

The deputies took one look at their wounded sheriff and opted to forgo the glory and admiration they could earn by rushing out into the brush and arresting the lawbreakers. A new man was elevated to the sheriff position, but he was way too smart to serve those warrants without a heap of help. Unfortunately, the deputies all had unbreakable appointments.

The city fathers shook down the store merchants for firearms and ammo, and with concentrated badgering shamed a posse of around thirty men to back Sheriff Brown in his hazardous undertaking. Sheriff Brown was a local and had a longtime acquaintance with Juan Cortina, so he had no problem leading his posse to the corrals of Rancho Santa Rita.

There was a problem when the men dismounted and tied their mounts to the rail fence, however. Sheriff Brown walked alone toward the house and called out to tell Juan that he had come to arrest him.

"Come out with your hands up!" Sheriff Brown called out in his most authoritative voice.

"Come and get me," Juan called back, above peals of laughter from his men.

Sheriff Brown turned to his posse, saw they were back in their saddles, and instructed them to dismount and follow him. Not one man moved, so Brown strode toward the house. A warning shot buzzed just above his head, and Brown hastily began to wave his white handkerchief. Bravely he walked to the yard gate and again told Juan that he was only obeying orders but that he had to make an arrest.

"You can trust me to see that you get a fair trial," Brown said, as Juan approached the gate from the yard side.

"Not with Stillman picking the jury," Juan chuckled. "No way will I surrender." Cortina then countered with his set of conditions, in lieu of being arrested. He handed Sheriff Brown a list of men who had wronged his people; they were all prominent citizens of the Brownsville area. There were lawyers, cattle barons, politicians, and contributors to the fund to hire Sheriff Shears. Juan wanted them arrested. In all, there were better than ten names. Brown studied the list as his posse turned their mounts and slowly disappeared into the brush in the general direction of Brownsville.

Not wanting to rile Juan Cortina, Sheriff Brown said that he'd see what he could do. His fear was that saying the wrong thing might trigger an attack on Brownsville. He folded the list with his warrants and put them into his pocket.

"I can't get these men together today," he finally said.

"When, then?" Cortina asked. "I'll give you three days."

Brown nodded his head in understanding, turned his horse, and returned to Brownsville.

Three days passed, then ten, as messengers delivered correspondence to and from Rancho Santa Rita. After thirty days messages were discontinued, and Brownsville citizens took deep breaths and began to dismiss the threat of Juan Cortina with disdain.

On September 30, however, their fear sprang back to life. A visitor from Brownsville, Red Thomas, was in Matamoros at Plaza de Benito Jaurez and was handed a printed handbill with a chilling offer that sent the businessman scurrying back across the river.

"Fellow Citizens," it read: "My part is taken! The voice of Revelations whispers, that to me is entrusted the work of breaking the chains of your slavery; that Our Lord will enable me to put our powerful enemies under foot, in compliance with the sovereign majesty—on my part I am ready to hold myself in sacrifice.

"A society is organized in Texas which devotes itself sleeplessly to exterminating tyrants—and driving the invading Americans back across the Nueces."

Juan Cortina's handbill proclamation went on to name names, and it rekindled fire from dormant embers of hatred for the Americans who peopled the Neuces Strip. Actually, the government of Mexico still disputed ownership of the land lying between the Neuces and the Rio Grande.

Red Thomas reported that the handbill had been circulating for some time and that the following of Juan Cortina grew larger by the day. He said that a strike on Brownsville could occur at any time and that it was definitely going to happen. Many of the named targets on Cortina's hit list vamoosed from Brownsville immediately.

Twenty-three years after Texans assumed they'd beaten Santa Anna and Mexico, Juan Cortina stormed the city of Brownsville, captured Fort Brown, which housed a detachment of the U.S. cavalry, and took charge of all government buildings and the city hall.

He released all the prisoners in the Brownsville jail and sacked the city, taking special pains to confiscate the property of the men who were named on his death list—attorneys William Hald, Francis Parker, J. S. Lake, O. Kelm, and Adolphus Gaevecke, along with the financial manager of his widowed mother. Most of those named had contributed the money to hire Sheriff Shears. They were all out of town when Cortina set up headquarters in the commandant's office.

Just after sunrise the next day, the Cortinistos finished their booty collection and threw a monumental victory celebration of barbecued cabrito washed down with a bountiful supply of mescal. They toasted the absence of the gringos who had been put to death as atonement for their crimes against Mexico and the Mexican population of the Neuces Strip.

Juan Cortina attended the gala celebration clad in an American colonel's uniform. He called a meeting of the townspeople and distributed a printed list of the men he wanted, and he demanded their delivery within the hour. "You will be rewarded with one hundred thousand dollars in American gold coin for each person you deliver," Juan continued. He informed the sparse gathering that if he was disappointed in the results, he would torch Brownsville and turn it to ashes.

Frantically, the Texans appealed to General Carvajal, who commanded the military in Matamoros. General Carvajal climbed into the saddle and personally led a force of *rurales,* foot soldiers, and dragoons to restore order and deal with Juan Cortina's threat.

Upon arrival, the Mexican force found Cortina's men preparing turpentine balls with which they planned to cremate Brownsville, Texas.

General Carvajal, who had a wide reputation for meaning precisely what he said, told Cortina to forget his turpentine balls or be prepared to face unpleasant circumstances. He also told him to remove the colonel's uniform, gather his drunken army, and get out of town.

Juan Cortina did as he was told, and he and his army returned to Rancho Santa Rita, but he had not abandoned his goal of dealing out tough times for the city of Brownsville. He posted his troops around the city, and no exit or entry was allowed to the beleaguered city without permission. He controlled the mail, and none was permitted to cross the Rio Grande. He intercepted all incoming steamers to Brazos Santiago and Point Isabel and upon the waters of the Rio Grande. Residents of Brownsville were systematically cut off from the outside world; they huddled in fear and awaited their doom. Cortina's men busied themselves robbing and pillaging area ranches, taking all valuables, and driving the cattle and horses away for future sale. To make matters worse, the numbers of Cortina's troops were still on the increase.

Red Thomas, a grizzled veteran of the brush country, managed to get across the Rio Grande and into the relative safety of Mexico. He made his way upriver two hundred miles to Laredo. He covered that distance in six days. He then dispatched riders to Corpus Christi and San Patricio and sent letters and wires pleading for help. Then he personally made the 150-mile ride to San Antonio in three days. He was the right man for the mission.

Relief forces began forming immediately. A Texas Ranger company commanded by Captain William Tobin headed out for Brownsville immediately and picked up additional gun hands along the trail. General Carvajal was again called to duty in Brownsville, and he and his troops set out to break Cortina's siege. The U.S. Army ordered troops to the area, and a force of volunteers formed themselves as the Brownsville Tigers.

The Brownsville Tigers tracked Cortina's army to a temporary headquarters within a few miles of Brownsville and engaged it in a skirmish. Juan Cortina feigned a retreat and lured the Brownsville Tigers into a trap. Slaughter preceded wild retreat, and the Tigers were badly beaten. The survivors limped back to Brownsville. They'd lost many rifles and a pair of cannons in the melee. Cortina's army had killed twenty of the Tigers and wounded many more. His forces were jubilant.

Companies of volunteers began to form in several Texas towns, and the liberators gathered at Palo Alto, but they too suffered defeat at the hands of Juan Cortina. Still, the allies did not quit the field. Cortina's soldiers regrouped around the middle of December, broke camp, left Rancho Santa Rita, and struck out to the north. They torched the ranch homes of Cortina's enemies as they made their march to Edinburg. They captured that small city and resumed their journey to Rio Grande City, 135 miles north of Brownsville.

They took over Rio Grande City on Christmas Eve of 1859 and demanded a hundred thousand gold dollars as ransom. To that time, Juan Cortina had captured two U.S Army forts, two cities, and several villages. He had a hundred thousand dollars in gold and livestock worth more than half a million. He had beaten the minions of law in the vast expanse of the Neuces Strip. He was pleased with his performance and designated Christmas Day as a fiesta day for his weary troops.

Unknown to the revelers as they collapsed into sleep and drunkenness following their feast and mescal, powerful forces were converging upon them. More than a thousand rangers, soldiers, and volunteers crept into position as the celebration waned and the full-bellied renegades collapsed into intoxicated rest. They were soundly beaten, much like their predecessors at San Jacinto, where Texas had captured Santa Anna and earned freedom for the Republic of Texas.

It was no longer safe for them to stay in Texas, but Juan and his men continued their raids and plagued the King Ranches and many others, along with survivors on his death list. He probably stole almost a million horses and cattle from Texas on those raids.

Ranger captain McNelly eventually wore the Contina gang out with persistent pursuit by a trained strike force. Cortina fled deeper into Mexico, disbanded his army, and went into politics.

He was elected mayor of Matamoros, later served as governor of Tamaulipas, and was instrumental in helping oust the French puppet Maximilian, who ruled Mexico for a time.

Juan Cortina was a warrior by nature but grew old and weary of battle. He campaigned for the presidency of Mexico and was beaten by Porfirio Diaz—a first cousin.

History deserted Juan Cortina at that juncture, but his memory still lives in the brush country of the old Neuces Strip.

High and Dry

When Texas and the Mexican armies went to war in 1848, the U.S. military took a hand in the proceedings, and one of their moves was the establishment of an outpost at Laredo.

Laredo is a goodly distance from the intersection of the Rio Grande and the Gulf of Mexico, but in that day and time the Rio Grande was not dammed every few miles, and scant water was siphoned off for irrigation and industry.

While the Rio Grande was on a rise from heavy rains up to the north, a U.S. Army steamship steamed up to Laredo and made a delivery. It dropped anchor, and the anchor stayed dropped for two years. The Rio Bravo del Norte had ebbed to a level insufficient to float a canoe.

As the war with Mexico raged about them, the crew of the steamer whiled away the days, weeks, months, and years waiting for rain in the north and enough of a rise to turn their boat around and float back to the Gulf.

To pass the time, the crew fished over the side for catfish by day and, clad in their civvies, did night duty investigating the attractions offered by Laredo, Texas, and the sister city of Nuevo Laredo across the river in enemy territory.

The possibility of being mugged and losing their money was not of a magnitude to keep that crew aboard after sundown. The cantinas furnished nightlife and served three-worm tequila, which served to enhance the charms of the señoritas at that impromptu naval operation in the desert.

Eventually, the water level rose, and the steamer rode the tide back to the Gulf of Mexico.

In years to come, the stories that crew of sailors told of their two-year trip up the Rio Grande probably fell on unbelieving ears.

Royal Flush

Once the ragtag army of Sam Houston had validated the claim of independence down in San Jacinto, by blindsiding Santa Anna's crack troops, who were observing siesta, the Republic of Texas got off to a start, but a mighty shaky one.

The ten-year span of the Republic featured management by four presidents. David G. Burnet led off and was followed by Sam Houston, Mirabeau B. Lamar, Sam Houston (encore), and Anson Jones.

On February 19, 1846, Texas was admitted to the United States, and a string of governors replaced the presidential parade.

They are listed in consecutive order for your edification and provide an opportunity for a little game to test your skill and knowledge of chief imported honchos from 1836. James Stephen Hogg of Rusk, Texas, became the *numero uno* of native-born, native-bred Texan governors in 1891, and our sons of Texas are not listed.

"Old habits die hard," as the saying goes, and when Jim Hogg vacated the Austin trough in 1895, we once again selected an east-of-the-Mississippi governor—Charles Allen Culberson. He was succeeded by Joseph D. Sayers, and then S. W. T. Lanham took the reins.

In 1907, another Texan "riz" to the top, and Thomas Mitchell Campbell served four years and was replaced by Oscar Branch Colquitt for a four-year run.

Pa and Ma Ferguson bestowed their legacy of Texas brand politics, off and on, from 1915 until 1935. Pa was impeached for skullduggery on August 25, 1917, but Ma seized the baton and pulled sporadic gigs from 1925 through 1935. Texas was blessed with two governors during the Ferguson era, since Ma let Pa run the show whilst she boiled the cabbage.

Then in 1939, Pappy Lee O'Daniel migrated to Texas, hired on, and peddled flour for Burris Mills. He originated the Light Crust Doughboys, serenaded rural Texas with stump-jumping music, and ran for governor. He received a majority of the vote—573,166—and totally eclipsed the cumulative total of the also-rans: Ernest O. Thompson, William McCraw, Tom F. Hunter, Karl A. Crowley, P. D. Renfro, Clarence E. Farmer, James A. "Pa" Ferguson, Marvin P. McCoy, Thomas Self, S. T. Brogdon, Joseph King, and Clarence R. Miller.

It was rare to find anyone who would admit to casting his ballot for Pappy, but he was governor all the same. He was a major disappointment, a crop failure, and he quit the job on August 4, 1941. He became a U.S. senator from Texas, and Coke R. Stevenson, a genuine Texan, took over and served Texas until 1947.

Native Texas sons and daughters continued to fill the job until Ann Richards had to relinquish the Texas throne to another non-native-born alien. Little George of the Bushwhackers got hisself elected to the presidency of these here United States in 2000, and the governorship served as his stepping-stone, just as with Pappy Lee.

Slick Rick from Paint Creek eased into the governorship as George struck out for Washington with his avowed ambition of wiping out evil and its practitioners.

Now then, the following is a consecutive listing of Texas's alien presidents and governors. Their states of export have been scrambled over at the right-hand side of the page.

You are hereby challenged to connect the man and the state origin. If you are able to do this, you probably know more about Texas politics than you should to enjoy good health, sanity, and peace of mind.

Give it a shot, and don't look for answers in the back of the book Just lie about your score if you've a mind to. It's the Texas way!

Presidents

David G. Burnet	Alabama
Sam Houston	Massachusetts
Mirabeau B. Lamar	Tennessee
Sam Houston (rerun)	Florida
Anson Jones	Iowa

Governors

J. Pickney Henderson	Ohio
George T. Wood	Kentucky
Peter Hansbrough Bell	Virginia
J. W. Henderson	Georgia
Elisha M. Pease	Arizona
Hardin R. Runnels	Rhode Island
Sam Houston (again)	New Jersey
Edward Clark	Oklahoma
Francis R. Lubbock	Michigan
Pendleton Murrah	Arkansas
Fletcher S. Stockdale	Indiana
Andrew J. Hamilton	Idaho
James W. Throckmorton	Utah
Elisha M. Pease	Montana
Edmund J. Davis	Hawaii
Richard Coke	North Dakota
Richard B. Hubbard	Washington
Oran M. Roberts	Maine
John Ireland	Connecticut
Lawrence Sullivan Ross	Delaware
Charles A. Culberson	North Carolina
Joseph Sayers	Oregon
S. W. T. Lanham	Louisiana
Oscar Branch Colquitt	New Mexico
W. Lee O'Daniel	Mississippi
George W. Bush	South Carolina

For the sake of symmetry, there are decoys listed among the states of choice. So be mighty careful—there are many traps for the unwary. Also, some states contributed more Texas presidents/governors than were really necessary. So be warned.

If the tabloid is correct in stating that "Inquiring Minds Want to Know," then you've got your work cut out for you. The correct answers are not printed in this book. You will have to look 'em up just like I did.

Lean Library

Mirabeau B. Lamar was a proud man on January 24, 1839, at the Third Congress of the Republic of Texas. It had taken a heap of doing, but he had prevailed in a matter that was close to his heart. He had been successful in convincing the Congress to appropriate ten thousand dollars for the establishment of the Texas Republic Library.

In 1980, the Mirabeau B. Lamar Library of the University of Texas at Austin had in excess of four million volumes, the largest library in the state and in the top ten of the United States. It is internationally known for its archives of twentieth-century British and American literature and more books on any subject you can name—or can be hauled in a flat bed wagon. An important addition during our sesquicentennial year was James Michener's 150-ounce *Texas: A Novel*. It features every word in the English language. Mirabeau, of course, never lived to see his namesake, but he would have admired the collection.

With the appropriation of the ten grand to buy books, there arose a problem—the republic was broke. Being president of a republic devoid of culture was bad enough, but having money promised for establishment of a library and then not getting the money was a bitter pill for Mirabeau to down. He made a big scene, and eventually $255 was made available to buy books. Mirabeau gave the princely sum to one of his trusted friends, who immediately set about the task of puttin' together a library for the republic.

The records of the search for and eventual purchase of the first books to grace the Library of the Republic of Texas is not available, but the resulting collection was probably the laughingstock of the republic and possibly the civilized world.

If Mirabeau had been considering reelection in 1841, he was barking up the wrong tree. His book-buying caper was all the ammunition old Sam Houston needed to get elected for his second term as president of the Republic of Texas.

An eighteen-volume set of the *Edinburgh Encyclopedia* was what was purchased for that $255.

And not another volume was added until nine years later, long after the republic had become the state of Texas.

Bluecoat Texan

Widow Davis and her eleven-year-old son Ed came to Texas from Florida in 1838. She settled in Galveston, and little Ed showed a propensity for law. He pursued his studies in Corpus Christi and passed the bar by avoiding the bars and applying himself to the books. He began his practice in Corpus, and later in Brownsville. Folk who recognized his talents predicted that he was destined for the governorship.

The Civil War loomed as a certainty, and Ed's sympathies lay with the South, so when a convention to consider secession from the Union was announced, he was hot to serve as a delegate.

Unfortunately, Ed was not chosen, and it really got his dander up. He didn't take the rejection well atall.

As a matter of fact, he kicked over the traces and metamorphosed into a wild-eyed Unionist. That decision didn't set too well with the rank-and-file citizenry, and Ed had to take it on the lam. He became a reverse wetback by putting the Rio Grande between him, his family, and the Texas Rebels. Once secession was a done deal and the fracas was picking up steam, Edmond Jackson Davis hustled a like-thinking regiment of Texans to oppose the Confederacy. His First Texas Cavalry was the first and most formidable Texas unit to fight under the Stars and Stripes.

Ed marshaled his troops in New Orleans and then moved to Galveston in the last month of 1862. They were looking for a few good men to swell their ranks, and Galveston was reported to be semi-unionist in their thinking. Such turned out not to be the case, so the First Texas Cavalry had to scatter and reconvene in Matamoros, Mexico. They felt they'd be safe in Mexico, but they were wrong.

A band of hard-case Texans, who referred to themselves as rangers, waded the Rio Grande, strung up one of the First Texas Cavalry soldiers, and had plans to hang the rest when they found the time.

A Mexican governor over in Tamaulipas interceded on behalf of Ed and his First Texas Cavalry and managed to save their necks by citing violation of the law of neutrality. The pro-South Rebels of Texas didn't like it much, but they turned the survivors loose. Davis wasted little time hustling his troops back to Louisiana, where they got back into the war and engaged the Confederates in a warm-up skirmish.

That acted as a trigger of confidence for the First Texas Cavalry, and they struck out for Galveston yet again. Their mission was to take Beaumont and the connecting railroad to Houston. They failed to get it done and once again had to vamoose to bayou country.

Then, one of the few instances of Yankee Texans against Rebel Texans ensued at Vermillion Bayou. There was no clear-cut winner in the battle, and statistics are not readily obtainable, but it did little to endear the unionist Texans to some of the folks back home.

The First Texas Cavalry ballooned to a force of seven thousand, and it was assigned to wrest control of the Rio Grande. It captured Ringgold Barracks at Rio Grand City and as a result of that success, Edmund Davis was elevated to command of all Federal cavalry in Texas and promoted to the rank of brigadier general.

When General Robert E. Lee began his retreat in Virginia in late 1864, it became obvious that the war was nearing the end, since the Union was prevailing on all fronts. The sons of the South were beaten, but neither side actually won. A sad chapter in U.S. and Texas history was concluded.

General Davis was dispatched to Galveston to negotiate surrender, and his First Texas Cavalry was mustered out after the U.S. Stars and Stripes was raised on June 5, 1865.

Back in civvies, Edmund J. Davis was urged to take the post of chief justice of the Supreme Court of Texas. General Phil Sheridan offered the job, but Edmund turned it down on the spot. He had bigger game in mind. The turncoat Texan had an ambition to be governor.

He was appointed as a delegate to the constitutional convention and acted as president of that body. He was favorable toward disfranchisement of all Confederates (including Texans), colored voting rights, and splitting Texas into three states. He failed to split up Texas, but his confidence had returned to prewar level, and he managed to get nominated for governor against Andrew Jackson Hamilton, who was also a former officer in the Union army.

Davis had powerful allies in the race. The military and the newly crowned president of the United States, General Ulysses S. Grant, were two of that number. With that backing, he won the election by a margin of eight hundred votes—the very first time the vote tally ever came out in his favor.

For four years Governor Edmund Davis tyrannized the citizens of Texas. He appointed eight thousand toadies to positions of power, created his own secret police force, and was a quick hand at announcing martial law when anyone got out of line. His reign was "famed" as the carpetbagger years. He enjoyed unlimited powers, which were conferred by the U.S. government.

Voters busted his bubble in 1873. Richard Coke bested him at the polls, and Edmund lost by forty thousand votes. He was smack dab back to his losing ways.

Tailored Texas

The Republic of Texas was born in a heck of a shape, and it remained in a heck of a shape until that shape was sanctioned by an act of Congress on December 19, 1846.

The geographic configuration was grotesque by any yardstick, since it included chunks of the present states of Colorado, Kansas, New Mexico, Oklahoma, and Wyoming. The Texas Panhandle was in Wyoming.

The financial shape of Texas was even worse. In 1846, a paper dollar would dwarf a wagon sheet, and a gold dollar was harder to come by than a front seat in heaven.

Federal troops organized a civil government way up north, and after the creation of Santa Fe County, New Mexico kicked over the traces and began to petition the federal government for recognition as a territory.

P. H. Bell was governor of Texas, and he rang out with disapproval. He stood ready to maintain Texas's claims "at all hazards and to the last extremity."

This impudence got old General Sheridan's hackles up, and being a man of choice words, he made no bones about his dislike for Texas and Texans.

Texans began a clamor for secession from the Yankee Union, and newspapers and the sentiment of mass meetings urged getting out of the "Union that embraces but to crush and destroy."

A stroke of genius surged through the White House, and a

nasty confrontation was narrowly averted. That same gambit has been used many times since and is as effective today as it was back then. Washington buried the problem under a mound of money. Texas received ten million dollars and the shape we recognize today.

Texans were pacified, since the money was sufficiently medicinal to ease the irritation. Besides, it was obvious that the new shape was handier for use on license plates.

Taxing Tale

James Knox Polk was born in Mecklenburg County of North Carolina on November 2, 1795. He was too honest to steal and too lazy to work, so he took up law and got into politics. Elected to the U.S. House of Representatives in 1823, he served there for fourteen years.

James'd just sit back until old Henry Clay took a position on some matter and then take the exact opposite stand. This habit made him a popular figure around Washington, and in 1839 he applied for and got a better job. He was elected governor of Tennessee.

After one two-year term, his popularity faded into near extinction. He lost a reelection bid in 1841. Two years later in 1843, he lost again, and his interest in Tennessee politics must have waned, because he turned his ambitions back to national office.

Van Buren was touted as a shoo-in nomination of the Democratic Party and was given a better than even chance to be the eleventh president of the United States. The party machinery began the grooming of James Polk as vice presidential running mate to Van Buren.

The annexation of Texas was a flaming issue, and delegates began to put the heat on Van Buren to see how he felt about admitting Texas into the Union. Naturally, Van Buren wanted to feel the way that would get him the nomination and the most votes. If he had a poll conducted, saw a fortune-teller, or flipped a coin, he got the wrong advice.

"I ain't gonna annex Texas into this here United States!" he declared.

Sitting back, James Polk sensed that Van Buren was sailing into the wind, and just like in the old days, he went the other way.

"I've always been foolish about Texas," he said. "If I were president I'd annex Texas in a New York minute! And I'm giving serious thought to making Mexico a state, too."

"James Knox Polk is a great American and a man after my own heart," said George M. Dallas.

Polk was elected president, and Dallas was his vice president.

While Texas was being annexed, Polk had a carpenter cut out foot-high individual letters from a two-inch walnut plank. The letters were placed on his desk, and they spelled out T-E-X-A-S.

When a visitor to his office sneeringly asked why in this world he'd been in favor of Texas's annexation, he'd smile, and rearrange his cut-out walnut letters to spell out T-A-X-E-S.

A House Divided

Dick Coke enlisted as a buck private at the beginning of the Civil War. He was a young lawyer down Waco way, having come to Texas from Williamsburg, Virginia, in 1850. His loyalty lay with the South, and he advanced to the rank of captain.

When taps sounded for the ending of hostilities, Dick journeyed back to Texas and was appointed to a district judgeship. Within a year he ran and was elected to the Texas Supreme Court.

General Phil Sheridan, who was in charge of Reconstruction and penance collecting in Texas, became alarmed at Governor Throckmorton and other pushy Texans who were attempting to reclaim the reins of state destiny. He removed both Governor Throckmorton and Dick Cole from office, judging them impediments to reconstruction. Neither man took the demotion very well, but Edmund J. Davis was installed as governor by the good General Sheridan.

The incident made Richard Coke mad enough to announce for governor in the 1873 election. Coke ran as a Democrat, with Edmund Davis representing the pride of the Republicans. It was round one in that historic string of contests betwixt the Ds and the Rs. Coke whupped Davis by a two-to-one margin.

It hurt Edmund's feelings to get bested, and he refused to turn the keys to the capitol over to a former Rebel scoundrel and urged President Grant to send troops to keep him on the payroll. Grant had more important things to tend to, and he told Davis as much and advised him to slink away and come on back up to Washington, D.C.

Davis decided he 'druther fight than switch, so he stationed a company of his freed slave soldiers on the ground floor to stand off any and all invaders of his kingdom. He directed military operations from the basement, but the Democratic forces would not be outfoxed. They got ladders and assembled on the second floor, convened the legislature, and swore Governor Coke into office.

Eventually, Davis gave up and along with his troops elected to vacate the bottom floor. It was an inglorious departure to be sure, but it got worse.

Judge John Ireland added injury to insult with a resounding kick to old Edmund's backside to aid him in getting down the stairs.

There's no way of knowing the full impact of that kick, but it was sufficient to get John Ireland elected governor of Texas in 1883.

Springtime in Luckenbach

Jacob "Jake" Brodbeck and his brother George got itchy feet back in 1846. Wurttemberg, Germany, their hometown, was a tad boring and too docile for young bucks who craved adventure and longed to see a little bit more of the world.

Jake was twenty-five at the time, and George was a little younger or perhaps a little older—but which is not all that important to this narrative. They booked passage, packed their belongings, and sailed away on August 25, 1846. Their destination was Texas.

Jake found work as a schoolteacher at Grape Creek, down in the Texas hill country, became a bona fide citizen in 1852, and six years later he and Christie Sophie Beherns got married. They devoted their efforts to increasing the population of Texas and collaborated in producing an even dozen copies before they broke the habit.

Jake served gigs as Gillespie county surveyor, county commissioner, and as a member of the school board when he wasn't helping Sophie boil diapers, and he still had time to pursue a lifelong interest in tinkering.

Back home in the old country, Jake had been good with his hands and had an interest in things mechanical. He'd once built a self-winding clock, which wouldn't, but in the early sixties the urge to build something welled up in him again.

Back when he was just a nubbin, he'd had an ambition to

build an airship, and he forthwith set about the project. By 1863, he had a scale model with wings and a rudder; it was spring powered and—best of all—it could fly.

"Wunderbar!" Jake said to Sophie, "Ain't that the beatinest thing you ever saw?" Sophie was burping the latest young 'un, and her enthusiasm was held well in check, but Jake paid scant attention at her lack of interest.

He relocated his tribe to San Antonio and hired on as a school inspector and found opportunities to show off his invention to the movers and shakers of the big city. His airship was a thing to marvel at in various exhibitions and fairs.

It didn't take long for Jake to interest three investors with money into backing his project. They were a Dr. Herff of San Antonio, a Mr. Guenther of New Braunfels, and Mr. Engel of Carnes

Mill. Jake set to work immediately, and toward the fall of 1865, he announced his labors were complete.

Long before Hondo Crouch, Willie, Waylon, and the boys' time, Jake set the test flight near Luckenbach on September 20, 1865, and the investors, along with Minny Moore, showed up to view the blastoff.

Jake wound his springs to the max, revved up, and sped down the runway. The airship rose to an altitude of twelve or fifteen feet and soared around a hundred feet before the spring gave up the ghost. Thence, an inglorious and noisy reunion with terra firma ensued precisely at altitude zero.

Jake went down with his ship, but he did not sustain near the damage that his airship did.

"I made a good landing," he may have said, "since any landing you can walk away from is a good landing." He dusted his britches and walked away.

Now Dr. Herff, Mr. Guenther, and Mr. Engel took the spectacle pretty hard, since the return of their monies depended on a patent sale. They admitted, to a man, that they were not interested in anteing any additional funds.

In desperation, Jake went up amongst the Yankee tribes in Michigan, but since winter was nigh he found only cold shoulders. Not only did Jake make a water haul, somebody stole his plans and blueprints. He returned to Texas and suffered a blue Christmas.

When Jake managed that flight in 1865, Wilbur was a sucking infant of two, and his brother Orville was not even on the ground up around Millville, Indiana.

As lads, Wilbur and Orville took a shine to mechanical and scientific pursuits. They flew kites like Ben Franklin used to do and folded gliders from sheets of eight and a half by eleven inch paper. They stayed at it before, during, and following puberty. In December 1903, they made four successful flights in an aeroplane of their design. Prior to takeoff, onlookers were intensely interested in the proceedings, and someone in the crowd asked the fledgling fliers if everything was in order.

"Everything's Jake!" Orville reported, which was an ancient expression that, over the years, mutated to today's "A-OK."

Despite rumors that the Wright boys had kinfolk over in Michigan, nobody could prove a thing.

They were on a roll, and the Wright brothers duplicated their amazing feat in Paris with Orville at the controls. The French Academy of Sciences hung a gold medal around his neck and kissed his cheek. Wilbur, of course, got the same treatment. Patent sales in France alone fetched a hundred grand, and that was a heap of money in them days.

There's no way of knowing how the news affected Jake, who'd made his flight thirty-eight years before the Wright boys, but on January 8, 1910, he was planted beneath the sod of his farm down near Luckenbach, Texas. Nobody knows whether he succumbed to sorrow, age, or too many kids.

Moral: Two Wrights can make a wrong.

Hog Wild

The sheriff was blindsided by five desperados who were in town to do a little shootin' and a lot of lootin'. The situation had the citizenry of Quitman on edge, along with the sheriff who sat on the edge of the chair he was tied to.

They were holed up in the county courthouse. The townspeople peered from store windows and from behind trees, but no one seemed to know what to do. So peering was the only action they were taking.

Then down the street came two grown men, led by a lanky stripling of a boy. He was armed with a rifle and led the way. Slowly but surely, they advanced toward the courthouse.

"Who's that kid out there in front?" a nail drummer asked the storekeeper in the hardware store where they shared a watching window.

"Why, that's Doc Shuford's hired hand. Jim is his first name. He's a printer's devil down at the newspaper I believe," the storekeeper replied after some thought. "He ain't been here in Quitman very long. They say he was orphaned when he was eleven. Came here from down around Rusk. Walked in barefooted to save his shoe leather."

The three men stopped in the street, and after a conversation, the five hard cases emerged with the hostage sheriff. A heated discussion ensued, and the young man suggested that they drop their guns and surrender to the sheriff.

"Ain't a man alive can take my gun," the outlaw leader snorted, "and I blamed sure ain't taking orders from no kid. I'm gonna take your rifle, sonny boy."

He was right. He took it right across his head and promptly dropped like an Otis elevator. Jim pointed the business end at the four who remained standing, and all the starch went out of them in a heartbeat. The sheriff collected their hardware, and with the help of the impromptu posse herded them all toward the jail. They had to carry their addled leader.

When the tide turned, outraged and suddenly brave citizens came running with rope in hand and announced themselves ready to perform their civic duty.

The good sheriff, with Jim's help, stood them off and sent them back to their stores and homes. All five prisoners were jailed without further difficulty, and they were jugged, tried, and sentenced to a few years of chopping sugar cane.

They harbored hard feelings toward the lad who'd stymied their taking ways, and the bandit leader swore blood vengeance upon his captor. Since they'd not killed anyone, their sentence was abbreviated. Later, at a party down in Van Zandt County, Jim was attacked by one or more of the desperados and almost lost his life.

Jim was employed as a typesetter, and he applied himself to the work and wound up owning his own newspaper. In addition, he studied law and was admitted to the bar in 1875.

Three years later he was elected county attorney of Wood County. Politics seemed to agree with him, and he moved up a notch and was elevated by the voters to district attorney of the Seventh Judicial District.

Jim set his sights a tad higher and rose to the post of attorney general of the state of Texas. He served two terms in that capacity, and Jim's dimensions increased right along with the weightier offices.

He won the nomination for governor in 1890 and ran the show from 1891 to 1895.

When Jim took the oath of office, he was forty-four years of age, and his metamorphosis from skinny kid was complete. He was still six foot two, but his tonnage had increased to 280 and some-odd pounds. His shadow reportedly weighed eight pounds, and he was offered a linebacker position by the Green Bay Packers. Of course, he refused the offer. He did not enjoy rolling around in the mud.

That was why he had a king-sized bathtub installed in the governor's mansion. "I mean to run a clean administration!" he's reported as saying. Most everyone referred to him as the "Big Governor" as he served his four years and retired undefeated.

James S. Hogg has yet another distinction that he will never relinquish, and it is not his height and/or weight figure.

He was the first native-born Texas to be elected governor of the Lone Star State—fifty-nine years after Texas won independence from Mexico.

Ma Knew Best

On Thanksgiving Day of 1925, Ma Ferguson was in the governor's box at College Station for the annual Longhorn-Aggie bloodletting, and she was sorely vexed by a loudmouth seated directly behind she and her entourage. Her husband, Pa, was also in the box with the group of Austinites, and he urged Ma to take names as he stoked her outrage with great pleasure.

Ma already had animosity in her craw, but the big-mouthed fan threw coal oil on the glowing embers with his boisterous behavior. When she got back to Austin, she penned a scathing admonishment and sent it posthaste to the individual who had caused her emotional turmoil at the "Big Game." She admitted later that she could not recall who won the game.

Her letter began on a somber note. She confessed that it pained her to have to write, but "what's right is right, and they ain't no two ways about it!"

Then she lit in with a vengeance and advised that she had been informed of a wingding perpetrated at a gathering of the Oil Men's Association in Fort Worth, Texas.

Although she did not personally behold the debauchery, she had reliable and unimpeachable information that her tormenter at the "Big Game" had "fitted up a building owned or controlled by you (perhaps a garage building) in the old-fashioned bar room way, providing a bar with the foot rail and the sawdust on the floor and behind the bar you had a man dressed in the old-fashioned bartender white apron style," for the Oil Men's Association in Fort Worth.

> To this place I am informed that you invited some 200 or 300 guests and to those who came, you dispensed drinks that were to say the least, stimulating and that you caused to be given away souvenir canes in which there is a hidden vial some 30 inches in length that contained approximately one pint of beverage.
>
> I have one of the canes in my possession which I am reliably informed came from your place. I am also informed that at said reception given by you many became stimulated and others were under the influence of an invigorating decoction, and that you in company with your guests participated in the consumption of the beverage.

To add insult to injury, Ma continued her letter to point out to her tormentor that he yelled "Hurrah for the Texas Aggies and Dan Moody!"

Dan Moody was attorney general for Texas and was conducting an investigation of the State Highway Department and the American Road Company concerning a matter of better than half a million bucks of tax money. Ma apparently disapproved of Dan Moody's behavior about as vehemently as she did of the bellicose attendee of the "Big Game." On the Saturday following Thanksgiving, she issued a proclamation offering a smooth five hundred bucks' reward for the conviction of any wealthy Texan who dared to violate state liquor laws.

Her letter continues:

> You, of course, remember your being in College Station on Thanksgiving Day of last week upon the occasion of the annual football contest between the A & M College and the University. If you do not remember, I can inform you that it was an imposing meeting of some 25,000 people from all parts of the state and there were thousands of young boys and girls, students and friends of both of these two great institutions, the pride of the state.
>
> I see from the papers that you admit that many times you cheered for Hon. Dan Moody and the A & M team. I can verify that you are correct in this statement as you were right behind the box that I was occupying, and on two occasions when you gave

vent to your vociferous exclamation you were only a few feet from me.

I believe your statement when you say in the papers that you were not aware of my presence and that you meant no personal discourtesy to me. Your friends who know you best assure me (and I believe them) that when you are in a normal condition that you are a courteous gentleman to the manner born, and I attribute your seeming affront to your unusual condition and the influence under which you were laboring at the time.

In your state it was natural for you to have been unable to distinguish between a colonel on my staff, dressed in khaki yellow, and a town policeman, dressed in blue, who under orders from the local authorities ejected you from the grounds in the interest of public peace. No member of my staff laid hands on you as suggested by you in the public press. Personally, I gladly forget any apparent discourtesy to me, as from my own observation I know you were not responsible at the time. But your actions involve a great principle and a matter of sound public policy, which I cannot overlook.

We have on the statute books a law against the unlawful sale, transportation or possession of intoxicating liquors. Also there is a law against intoxication in public places.

It will not be denied that the foundation of our civilization is our educational institutions. In and around these temples of knowledge from the country school to the college and the university we seek to teach the rising generation the virtue of morality, sobriety and correct living. It is here that the proper precepts and example is set or should be set before the young boys and girls that will aid them to become good citizens. These simple truths are so self-evident that to state them is to prove them.

If those in charge of the management and direction of our educational institutions shall by their personal deportment display those vices that are repugnant to the idea of strict morality and sobriety, then such results in the students of these institutions can not be expected.

If as head to the board of the Texas Technological College you reserve to yourself the right to appear in a public place in the condition you were in at College Station on Thanksgiving Day, then every student who saw you could justify him or herself for doing the same thing. If a student at Tech College should appear on the Lubbock campus as you appeared in College Station the faculty would promptly expel such student from the college. And yet in such case the student could plead your case and the example and the precedent set by you in justification. If the heads of our institutions cannot practice and preach sobriety, then our hopes for educated citizenship are in vain and useless. . . .

I plead for a better example for our boys and girls. You have set a standard that cannot be tolerated. For the good of the public service I emphatically affirm that you should send me your resignation.

Miriam A. Ferguson,
Governor of Texas

As you may have detected, Governor Miriam Amanda Ferguson was almighty displeased with the antics of another fan at the titanic struggle between the UT Longhorns and the Texas Aggies on Thanksgiving Thursday in 1925.

She knew firsthand of the wages of sin, or as she and Pa claimed, "the suspicion of sin." Pa, you see, was close to impeachment back in 1917. He was accused of artful uses of campaign contributions from certain breweries. He banked goodly sums in a private bank account and then refused to pay the state taxes on the accumulated interest. Pa claimed innocence in the matter. When heat for his questionable tactics reached a three-digit temperature, he threw in the political towel and began to groom Ma. She was elected in 1925 and pulled one hitch.

The bigmouth that got her hackles up was the publisher of the *Fort Worth Star-Telegram*. He was a swashbuckling type, who reportedly claimed that Fort Worth was situated, "where the pavement ends and the west begins." His name was Amon Carter.

Pass the Biscuits, Pappy

Wilbert Lee O'Daniel found work with a flour-making outfit as soon as he finished school up Kansas way. He wasn't much of a hand in the manufacturing, but he developed into a flour peddler of distinction.

He hired on with Burrus Mills after his migration to Fort Worth in 1925, and by 1928 he'd risen like the product he pushed. He took charge of the company's radio advertising, began jingle and song writing, and put together a western swing band he dubbed the "Light Crust Dough Boys" (from Burrus Mills). His popularity spread like mistletoe, and in 1935 he started his very own flour company. Imagine, if you can, what his band may have looked like had it been the Pillsbury Dough Boys.

W. Lee "Pappy" endeared himself to the rural Texas of that day and time with his inspirational and religious crusade to improve mankind with higher goals and better flour.

"You art to run for governor," a fan opined at one of Pappy's performances. Pappy liked the sound of "Governor O'Daniel" and decided to make a run for it. He announced, with old-age pensions, the Golden Rule, and white-flour biscuits as the planks of his platform. His campaign was not unlike a traveling medicine show, excepting the product he was pushing.

Twelve other candidates were seeking the governorship in the race for 1938, and that dozen aspirants laughed and derided the antics of Pappy Lee O'Daniel. They quit laughing when the votes were all tallied though—Pappy beat 'em like a drum. He got a cool reception from the legislature when he reported for duty down at Austin, and most every program he'd promised his Populist followers failed miserably.

A goodly number of those legislators went down for the count in the next election, and Pappy's following remained loyal. He waged merciless warfare on communism and academic extremists at the University of Texas and made life miserable for anybody that opposed his way of thinking.

Pappy wearied of butting his head against the proverbial stump, and he resigned state politics on August 4, 1941. He had bigger game in mind and announced his ambition to be a U.S. senator.

In a special election in 1941, he squared off against Lyndon Baines Johnson for the coveted position. Pappy bested the young whippersnapper from the brushy wilds of central Texas. Pappy tanned his hide and packed his bags for Washington, D.C.

Lyndon licked his wounds and bided his time until the next round. He also went down to Jim Wells County to meet with the kingmakers of South Texas. He was taken in as a blood brother, and when he got back home he told Lady Bird that he'd changed his luck.

"You just wait until 1948!" he said. And of course you know how that turned out.

Pappy tried for a comeback as Texas's *jefe grande* in 1956 and 1958, but the old magic had departed him. No longer was there any life in the movement to amend a Texas slogan to "Six Flags and a Flour Sack Over Texas," but Pappy has one distinction that differentiates him from all politicians of the Texas persuasion.

In his career of public service, not once did he cast a vote for himself! Or for anybody else, for that matter.

He refused to pay a poll tax.

The Four-Bit Governor

Dick Hubbard carried a lot of weight and cast a shadow that covered a fair size area, but he was squashed in seeking another term at the Democratic Convention of 1878. He taxed the scale with his three hundred pounds, but his administration was sullied by the feudin', fussin', and fightin' of some members of his constituency.

Juan Cortina did most of his shopping east of the Rio Grande, where it was conducted mainly on the honor system, which was Juan's short suit. The Taylor-Sutton feud in southwest Texas and the Mitchell-Truit feud on the Brazos were diversions from the Salt War out near El Paso. Ben Thompson and King Fisher were gunned down around San Antonio and Sam Bass absorbed an overdose of lead at Round Rock. Texas was on a tear, and of course Dick Hubbard was blamed, and fried in his own fat.

He offered his services for a second term, but a former governor, J. W. Throckmorton, submitted his credentials, along with Colonel W. W. Lang, who was a high muck-a-muck in the Farmer's Grange. Neither aspirant was able to amass a majority, so a thirty-two-member committee of Democrats was given the awesome task of making a choice. They did, on a fourth ballot, but they opted for neither of the above. Instead, they ran in a ringer. It was Judge Oran Milo Roberts, who was a battle-scarred veteran of tacky politics.

As a matter of fact, he'd been elected as a U.S. senator back in

1866, but the Republican majority had told him they didn't have a place for him to sit or a chair to spare for a Texas Democrat—especially one that had written the oath of allegiance to the Confederacy, when Texas joined up with the Southern Rabble. To emphasize his feelings at that time, he had also raised an infantry regiment, in which he pulled a little time as the colonel. He was a short-timer as a soldier and went home to a higher calling. He was chief justice of the Supreme Court of Texas until the war ended. The carpetbaggers removed him from his office and advised him to "judge not."

When word of his nomination reached old Milo over in Tyler, he rode into town on a pinto pony, borrowed fifty cents from a friend, and sent a telegram accepting the nomination. He told them to save a chair if he happened to win. That four bits was his total ante for the governorship.

Milo received 158,933 votes and totally eclipsed A. B. Norton, a Republican who only managed 23,402 votes. The Greenback Party choice, Joe D. Sayers, ran a distant second with 55,002 backers.

Milo's reputation of "throwing pennies around like they were manhole covers" did not suffer any damage when he assumed the Texas governorship. He lowered taxes and swung the deal for construction of the Texas capitol building by swapping West Texas mesquite groves for materials and labor. He also peddled public lands to unwary developers in order to finance the public debt. He became the "pay as you go" man and was elected to a second term.

Sure, he swapped three million acres of prime real estate in return for turnkey construction of the state capitol—but can you guess whose ownership the mineral rights are vested in? He also deeded sixteen sections per mile to the builders of the rail lines that crisscross Texas. Milo understood horse trading and getting more bang for the buck. In his second term, he reduced the tax rate from fifty cents on the hundred to thirty.

Milo's initial investment in the governor's position, you'll recall, was four bits and for that sum he received 158,033 votes. That figures out to a cost of $0.000003 per vote.

Jekyll-Hyde Governor

Allan Shivers inherited the governor of Texas title when Beauford Jester passed on in July 1949, and he enjoyed the job, apparently. He still holds the title for endurance at that post. His reign began July 11, 1949, and lasted until 1957, which works out to three and a half terms.

When his abbreviated term ran out in 1950, Shivers diligently sought reelection, and he trounced the Republican candidate Ralph Currie by a vote of 335,010 to 39,737. In those days, there were barely enough Republicans in Texas to bait a trotline. Some will tell you that's what shoulda happened.

When 1952 rolled around, Allan drew stiff opposition from Ralph Yarborough, who made three runs for governor; he lost three times too, but eventually got a gig in the U.S. Senate as consolation prize. Shivers beat Ralph by an almost two-to-one margin and then performed a miracle for that day and time—he had the nomination of both the Republican and Democratic Parties. He received 1,375,547 Democratic votes and managed 468,319 from the Republicans. It is not known which primary Allan voted in or which ticket he marked in the general election. Once the Democratic planks were adopted, if he voted Republican he lost his own vote but still won the governorship.

When he ran in 1954, Ralph was back, and the score wound up with Allan leading by 22,919 votes, but in the second round Shivers blitzed old Ralph by a 775,088 to 683,132 tally. Then

Allan blew the Republican aspirant Tod Adams plumb out of the tub. Tod only got 66,154 nods of approval, and if you recall, old Allan got almost half a million Republican votes back in 1952.

When 1956 rolled around, Allan Shivers decided he'd had enough and, refusing another run, put himself out to pasture. The only governor of Texas who lost the vote and won the governorship by the unparalleled strategy of splitting himself and running as both a Republican and a Democrat.

Hanging chads, dimples, and the Supreme Court were not at all involved.

Medicinal Purposes

Lyne T. Barrett brought in Texas's first oil well on September 12, 1866. The site was near Melrose in Nacogdoches County, and Mr. Barrett had exercised a good deal of patience before completing his strike. He'd held the lease for the duration of the Civil War, since it was hard to hire hands with the war on and all. He did, however, pay his lease renewal fee on October 9, 1865.

His drilling machine was in the principle of a huge brace and bit, and was activated by a steam engine. He used hog lard to lubricate the moving parts. His apparatus huffed and puffed to a depth of 106 feet, and from that pay zone Mr. Barrett was rewarded with an ocean of the smelly, black substance. He swung into full production, ten barrels a day, and before many days he'd filled half the fruit jars and all the whisky barrels in the county. He had oil enough to meet the existing need of the universe, and it is worth noting that old Lyne single-handedly engineered the very first oil glut.

Folk around the county would go miles out of their way to make sport of Mr. Barrett's oil operation. It was embarrassing to his family, but Lyne Barrett didn't care; he kept his well in full production. With composure rare in humankind, Lyne Barrett endured the mindless ribbing by those misguided people, and eventually his big break came like a clap of thunder!

Martin Meinsinger of Brownwood became a successful drummer of petroleum products in 1878. He peddled them as a lubricant and found buyers willing and able to lay down four bits for a gallon.

For the ailing, he bottled it and labeled it for internal combustion. In the bottle, it was an unequalled treatment for rheumatism, all manner of stomach disorders, and it was invaluable for treating burns, cuts, and open sores. Some claimed it cured baldness and that it was a match for the most advanced case of dog mange.

As medicine, it was offered in four-ounce bottles, and you could buy as many as you needed at two bits each.

A rival product suffered a wane in popularity, and most snake oil drummers fell into bankruptcy.

Langtry Legend

Judge Roy Bean, the law west of the Pecos, was an enterprising ingenious fellow, who worshiped the beautiful Lily Langtry.

On February 21, 1869, he promoted and staged a world heavyweight championship bout between Bob Fitzsimmons and Peter Maher. Fitzsimmons was the American champion, and Pete was the best scrapper in Ireland. The match had been outlawed in both Texas and Mexico, but Roy Bean was not distressed. He'd've taken the Mike Tyson–Lennox Lewis comedy.

He located a sandbar in the middle of the Rio Grande, just below Langtry, and it was there that a ring and bleachers were erected to accommodate the titanic struggle for the heavyweight championship of the world.

Much of the sand for that bar came down the Pecos from as far away as New Mexico, but Roy Bean judged that it was no man's land once it was on deposit in the Rio Grande.

Lumber for ring and seating construction was, no doubt, imported, but records are sketchy concerning its point of origin and cost. Cost is probably least important, since Judge Roy ruled that the materials were of inferior quality and refused to pay for them.

Many of those in attendance were standing in the tequila and taco lines as the combatants were introduced, the bell sounded, and that memorable struggle commenced.

Bob Fitzsimmons, eager to get back home, decked Pete Maher at a minute and a half of the first round.

Pete hit the floor and stuck like a Band-aid.

Grumbling, the crowd repaired to the mainland and the Vinegaroon Saloon for a long wait for the first train out.

Until now, Judge Roy Bean's real motive for promoting this monumental athletic competition had been shrouded in mystery. Contrary to common belief, it was not for the money!

The match was nothing more than a ploy to lure Lily Langtry to the town named in her honor. The judge implored her to attend the fisticuffs and render "The Star Spangled Banner."

Lily turned him down, with the explanation that she was having her hair done that day.

Hanging Out

J. W. "Choctaw" Robinson owned and operated a sawmill, which was the main business around Hazel Dell back around 1867. Mr. Robinson was also a Baptist minister, and his two callings were the creation of straight boards and straight and narrow conduct. He chose an unlikely environment in which to practice his latter craft.

The Hazel Dell settlement was in the southeast corner of Comanche County where FM 591 and FM 1702 intersect. (Farm to Market 1702 is located between Dublin and Comanche, on State Highway 36.) Some say that the name was chosen for the hue of the soil and the valley surrounding the site. Actually, an early settler who liked the "Hazel Dell" hymn suggested the community title.

Choctaw Robinson was one of the earliest emigrants, but he had little in common with the other early arrivals. The rough-and-tumble cowboys led the way, but the criminal element was close behind. Horse and cattle rustlers, murderers, gunslingers, and real estate swindlers made their appearance around 1870, and business picked up in Hazel Dell.

Comanche County at that time was the jumping-off place to cross the big dry and make a run for El Paso or the New Mexico Territory. The front line of expanding civilization is almost always preceded by the driftwood of humanity. One step ahead of the law and owners of fast horses was a quick description of the early arrivals to Hazel Dell.

Once the genuine settlers, cowmen, and farmers arrived and outnumbered the crooks, the crooks moved on in search of new territory. That was generally true of the westward expansion of Texas and the United States of America as a whole.

Gunplay and rope stretching became the major activities around Hazel Dell; legend has it that nine of the first ten inhabitants died violent deaths. Choctaw Robinson was the only holdout, and it was most likely due to his occupation—and his ability to say words over the fallen when ground was broken to receive them.

A Mr. Stone partnered in a general store with a man called Priedo. They decided to sell their business and inventory, buy cattle, and herd them north, where there was profit to be made.

As the money accumulated, Priedo did his math and figured out that he'd make twice the profit if he owned the whole herd and didn't have a partner. He hired an Indian who was in the business to snuff Mr. Stone. The contract was executed, along with Stone, and the contractor pocketed his money and high-tailed it out of Hazel Dell. Nobody went looking for him.

Ben Mackey was a heavy drinker and noted hell raiser in Comanche County, and he liked to practice his art in George Conway's saloon. Ben and George disagreed on something or the other, and Ben drew his trusty six-shooter and put a third of his load in George's direction. George was unharmed, since he was quick on his feet and was able to dodge both bullets. Ben was about to launch round three when the bartender, a man named Hogue, put a shot through Ben's neck. Ben's shot put a hole through the ceiling. The Mackey clan was notorious and numerous, so Hogue resigned his barkeep job and vamoosed with all due alacrity. Nobody went looking for him, either.

Bill Jefferies rode by horseback to the Head home and called out to W. D. McFall, who was visiting his father-in-law. When McFall stepped from the porch, Bill cut him down with a buffalo gun.

Mr. Head came out with guns blazing, and Jefferies headed for the tall timber. Nobody went after him, but Bill and his brother Nute ran out of luck not long after. The brothers were taken from the Meridian jail and strung up by an aroused citizenry.

A group of Hazel Dell residents formed a vigilante force to try and stem the crime wave and reign of terror to which the area was being treated. Lawmen were hopelessly outnumbered, and sometimes they had to sleep. Volunteers took the night shift, and they did not discriminate due to sex, age, or national origin. To them a crook was a crook and deserved to be straightened by being suspended from an oak branch with a stout hemp rope.

Take the Frailey boys for instance—a sixteen-year-old and his twenty-one-year-old brother. Officers of the law apprehended them in the theft of some cotton over around Lamkin. They were chained together and locked in the room of an empty store at Hazel Dell. A torrential rainstorm made it chancy to get them any farther toward the jailhouse at Comanche until morning.

Thirteen men, all wearing black slickers, black masks, and mounted on black horses persuaded the officers to agree, at gunpoint, to a change of custody. Daylight and a search party located the two boys within a quarter-mile of town, hanging side by side and still handcuffed together. They were planted side by side, still handcuffed, according to legend. Legend further claims that on dark and rainy nights strange and eerie lights could be seen at the site of the lynching. *¿Quien sabe?*

Of the original first ten settlers to arrive in Hazel Dell, six were hanged and three were shot. Reverend J. W. "Choctaw" Bill Robinson was the only man to leave town with the forked end down.

Pike's Pique

Jim Pike came to Texas in the spring of 1859. He hailed from Ohio, where he had hired out to deliver twenty head of horses to Dallas. They were stolen horses, but Jim apparently was not apprised of that tidbit of information by his employer until he was in the saddle and ready to head for Texas. He and the man who had hired him looked at each other over drawn guns, and Jim did not blink. The other fellow put his pistol back into its scabbard.

"I hired you to take them horses to Texas for me," he said. "You didn't ask me where I got them, and I've paid you to make the drive. So what's the matter with you? Are you yellow?"

Jim Pike lowered his gun and assured his employer that he was not at all afraid but that he didn't like to be lied to. Even if the lie was an omission of fact. He turned his horse and struck out for Texas. He saw the horses into the designated corral in Dallas and, liking what he'd seen on his journey, decided to look around Texas for a job. He was a printer by trade and decided to try his hand down Austin way.

When he arrived he was alerted to the need for young men with grit enough to help in the struggle to curb lawlessness in the central Texas area. Indians were a constant threat to domestic tranquility, and matters were worsened by the fact that between hostilities the raiding parties merely retreated for R and R to their reservation up in Oklahoma. His ambition to be a typesetter was abandoned on the spot.

Pike's first mission was the pursuit of a marauding band of Indian horse thieves, and he acquitted himself with such nerve and daring that he was urged to sign on with the Texas Rangers. He was willing, able, and eager to accept the invitation.

On a mission up the Brazos, his ranger company had several brushes with a band of roving Indians before engaging in a full-fledged showdown with a Comanche band under the command of Chief Katampsie.

According to Pike's report of the incident, thirteen of the rangers were preparing stewed venison when around a hundred Comanche braves, painted for battle, charged into the ranger camp. As the rangers ran for cover near an abandoned house, the Comanches charged, but the straight-shooting rangers decimated them by felling seven Comanches.

The rangers, cornered near the house, were surrounded by circling Comanches on fleet horses. Since horses were a bigger target than riders, the rangers shot the mounts, and twenty of the marauders were reduced to pedestrians. The bruised-up braves hot-footed it to a ravine, still within range of the beleaguered ranger battalion, and sniped from their cover. As a measure of the firing's intensity, fourteen hundred bullet holes were later counted in the house.

The battle raged on for twenty-four hours before reinforcements for the ranger troop rode in from Caddo, and the tide of battle shifted, with the edge now belonging to the rangers.

At that juncture, a white man appeared and demanded that the Indians cease firing. They did. Major Lieper, Indian agent in charge of the Oklahoma reservation, chided the renegade Indians for their tacky behavior and ordered them back to their allotted area. They griped a little, but they obeyed the major and departed the scene.

Then the bruised and battered rangers got their licks in on Major Lieper. Pike was by nature a hot-tempered man, and his anger was at near Pike's pique level. The major told them that a fine for leaving the reservation would be levied on the entire reservation as punishment for the deeds of the AWOLs. Captain Knowlin, who headed up the rangers, insisted on extracting a food penalty by going into the camp and claiming flour, bacon, and corn from Chief Katampsie. After some argument, the agent agreed to terms.

"You've got a mighty poor way to operate a reservation," Pike added.

Pike insisted on being one of the three rangers to go into the camp and collect the foodstuffs, and while it was being loaded, the old chief vowed vengeance. The rangers drew their weapons as he ranted and raved, which quieted him down to a whisper. The three men left camp with their booty.

Pike quit the rangers when secession was inevitable. His sympathies and loyalty lay with the Union, and he was one of but a handful who voted against secession. He left Texas, enlisted in the Union army, and managed to survive the conflict, but he did not return to Texas.

He remained in the army after war's end and was stationed on the western frontier when his fort was attacked by hostile Indians.

The soldiers grabbed their rifles and rushed to their defense positions.

Pike's rifle jammed, and in his fury, he smashed it to the ground. The cartridge exploded and shrapnel caused his death.

Jim Pike died by his own hand, but it could not be classified as suicide. He let his violent temper gain the upper hand one time too many.

The First Fifty

The Republic of Texas did not enjoy an easy birth. Texans by choice anted their lives at the Alamo and at Goliad, and if they'd been faint of heart, they would have turned tail and made a run for the border. That was not the option they chose, and a small patchwork force humbled the military might of Mexico at San Jacinto. They earned independence the old-fashioned way—they fought for it! To the amazement of the world, they won. The Republic of Texas rose and stood on its own two feet for ten long years, waiting impatiently for admission to the United States of America, and those ten years were no walk in the park.

They endured constant harassment from Indians and the sore losers to the west of the Rio Grande, but they stood strong and gained membership into the Union in 1845 and became its twenty-ninth member.

The War between the States, or more popularly the Civil War, disturbed a brief complacency and relative peace for the young state, and Texas cast its lot with the Confederacy. Texans seceded from the Union they had so arduously sought, and they wound up in the loser's bracket.

The woes and hardships inflicted upon the Confederacy were harsh, and Texas was recipient of its fair share. The Texans paid penance with suffering and hardship, but they paid in full and earned forgiveness and a second chance at being a state in good standing in the United States of America.

© chupp '02

Upon the celebration of its first fifty years, Texas had been a republic, a state in the Union, a Rebel state of the Confederacy, and had worked its way back into the Union.

The fiftieth birthday honored the heroes who had perished in the struggle for independence and the survivors who had kept the faith and helped Texas survive and mark that anniversary. The road Texas had traveled had been rough and rocky, but the journey had been completed and hopes were high for better things to come. The "betters" came from time to time, but so did the "worses."

G.T.T.

Jim Courtright was fabricated of equal amounts of the good, the bad, and the ugly. He was, according to those who knew, as gifted as Bill Hickok, William Bonny, Wyatt Earp, or Bat Masterson in the art of the quick draw and pinpoint accuracy when the chips were down.

Jim's youth is shrouded in mystery, but it is known that he was born in Iowa in 1848. He served in the Civil War, under the command of General John Logan, and came through the war without a scar. He returned to Iowa but found life there not to his liking and decided to emigrate to a livelier locale. He marked his departure by painting a succinct message on his front door. He lettered his announcement "G.T.T." Translated, it was his message to Iowans. The letters stood for "Gone to Texas."

Courtright was taller than average and towered over most citizens of Fort Worth when he hit town. He shunned barbershops, and his shoulder-length black hair coupled with his height made him easy to locate in a crowd.

He also wore a revolver on each hip and was adept at drawing with either hand, or simultaneously if the occasion demanded. He was as fast as a coiled rattler and just as deadly. The gravest situation only increased his speed, coolness, and accuracy. He was a gifted dealer of death—ideal qualifications for an army scout, and in his army days General Logan had put Jim on the payroll in that capacity and had had him range over northwest Texas, New

Mexico, and Arizona. General Logan was never disappointed by his choice.

So it was that Jim, wearied of too many miles in the saddle and the loneliness of his occupation, resigned from the army and rode to Fort Worth. Fort Worth was a wild town, and Jim's credentials got him the job of city marshal. He served faithfully and well in that position until he made a bad choice in politics. He selected the weaker faction to side with and lost his job at election time.

Around that same time, Colonel A. J. Fountain was dickering with Texas Ranger Jim Gillett out in El Paso. Colonel Fountain was a major player in New Mexico politics, and he was earnestly seeking a man to curb the uproar at Lake Valley Mining Camp, near Rincon in New Mexico. Lake Valley was a place where the bars and bordellos operated around the clock, and a tougher-than-nails marshal seemed to be the only option. Colonel Fountain came to El Paso to proposition Texas Ranger Gillett, who was qualified to see that law and order was enforced at Lake Valley.

"Sign on," Colonel Fountain said, "and we'll pay twice what you're drawing as a ranger. I know the job you've done here in El Paso and that you're the man for my new job."

It was an attractive offer, and Gillett thought it over carefully, but he decided to refuse. He confessed that he planned to get out of law enforcement and try his hand at raising cattle. "I'm tired of the strain and danger in the law business, but I do appreciate the offer."

Colonel Fountain was disappointed but not much surprised. He also knew Gillett's reputation for sticking to his decisions. He tried another tack and asked Gillett if he had knowledge of a man who might measure up.

Gillett did not hesitate to name Jim Courtright. Gillett said that he'd seen and worked with the best of hired guns and that Courtright was the equal of John Wesley Hardin or Ben Thompson. He also pointed out that Jim Courtright worked on the right side of the law. "He was marshal down in Fort Worth," he added. "I'll wire him for you if you'd like me to."

Jim Courtright came to El Paso and quickly struck a deal with Colonel Fountain. He traveled to Lake Valley immediately. Fountain accompanied Jim and introduced him around the camp, and the new marshal settled into the job.

There were two men who had discovered that stealing ore was less strenuous than digging, and not wishing to give up their chosen line of work, they made the mistake of challenging Jim Courtright. Jim prepared them for admission to Boot Hill with two well-placed shots and announced to the miners that he had plenty of ammunition left for thieves and troublemakers. Lake Valley became a law-abiding town, and those who disagreed were either buried or relocated themselves to another geographic area.

Jim got bored with his job after a while and welcomed an offer from his old friend, General Logan. The general now owned and operated a sizable ranch in American Valley, New Mexico, and he had a problem that he felt might be right down Courtright's alley. The problem was squatters. They were settling in ever increasing numbers, and they put fences around their land to keep the free-ranging cattle out of the pea patch.

The ranchers claimed the range and water by reason of pre-emption, but the sodbusters maintained that they had every right to fence and protect public lands. The title to land depended mostly on whoever could take and defend it. The cattlemen decided that their rights were rooted in the Grandfather Clause, even though it was not written on paper.

Jim Courtright hired on at premium wages and set about thinning out the settlers. He served notice that they would be wise to pack their belongings and move on. Jim hired Jim McIntyre, of Texas Panhandle reputation, as his well-armed and able assistant in emigration procedures.

Two settlers had taken up occupancy of choice tracts on the Logan Ranch, and they chose to defy Courtright and McIntyre. It was a grave error in judgment.

Those settlers were well known and liked by most folk in the American Valley, who did not even raise cattle. Warrants were issued for the arrest of Courtright and McIntyre by the governor of New Mexico. Both men were charged with murder. They lit out for Fort Worth, where Courtright felt he would not be easily located, but McIntyre was not so sure. He booked passage to South America.

New Mexico authorities, however, sent an arresting officer to Fort Worth, and he had warrants issued by the governor of Texas for the arrest of both men. Officer Richmond enlisted the help of Lieutenant Grimes and Corporal Hayes of the Texas Rangers to accompany him in the arrest of Jim Courtright. The arrest was made October 18, 1884, and Richmond's behavior in the matter was not accorded much respect around Fort Worth.

Texas Adjutant General King stated that Richmond's actions were reprehensible and not justified by Courtright's alleged crime. Residents and friends of Fort Worth were indignant, and their sympathies were with Courtright. Public sentiment was that Jim Courtright was being railroaded for a hanging in New Mexico.

When Courtright was taken to the Union depot to board a westbound train, a huge crowd showed up, and its mood was not festive. The Texas Rangers managed to handle the incident without bloodshed, but Courtright did not board the train. On the authority of Judge Hood of District Court, he was placed in the county jail instead.

Word of an attempt to free Courtright reached Austin, and the governor ordered Adjutant General King to Fort Worth with the directive to maintain order and execute the law. While King was en route, Courtright escaped, and Richmond was charged with misconduct and folly.

He had taken Courtright from his cell and escorted him to a restaurant on Main Street for his evening meal. They were accompanied by two Texas Rangers. The cafe was alive with Courtright sympathizers, and the reason became obvious once the diners were seated. Courtright arose with a Colt revolver in either hand and announced that he'd lost his appetite and would be leaving early. His friends had hung the revolvers on nails under the tabletop where Jim was to be seated.

He backed out the door where his saddled horse awaited, and as he rode away the crowd persuaded the rangers to refrain from pursuit. King conducted an investigation, and both rangers were found blameless in the escape.

Jim Courtright went to South America. Eventually, the heat subsided, and Jim returned to Fort Worth and quietly surrendered to authorities. A jury was empaneled, the case was heard, and Jim Courtright was acquitted of all charges.

Jim formed the TIC Commercial Detective Agency of Fort Worth, but despite the respectable title, it was merely a shakedown operation, collecting protection money from gamblers and saloon keepers. Jim Courtright got into racketeering and collecting protection money from less than legitimate business enterprises. His reputation with a gun was a powerful incentive for being a dues-paying member in good standing. Jim Courtright had descended to questionable depths.

Luke Short arrived in Fort Worth via stopovers in Leadville, Colorado, Tombstone, Arizona, and Dodge City, Kansas, and each move had not been far in front of the law. He promptly opened a saloon and gaming establishment. True to his family name, Luke was a short stub of a man, but he could operate a big gun and refused Courtright's invitation to enroll in the TIC protection program.

At their initial meeting, Luke had his armed employees strategically scattered around the barroom, and Jim Courtright left mad and disappointed but in one piece.

Luke Short was a native Texan, and he was armed and danger-
ous, too. His ability to put a bullet hole between the eyes of his
adversaries had earned him the title of "Undertaker's Friend." He
operated the White Elephant Saloon on Fort Worth's north side,
and he not only rudely refused to buy insurance from Jim Courtright, but instructed him to go and jump in the Trinity River. For
the first time in his life, Jim Courtright had to back down.

Jim's pride and reputation would not allow him to accept that
defeat, and before many days had passed, he was back in front of
the White Elephant extending an invitation to Luke Short to come
out and talk. Luke had no choice other than compliance. His reputation was also on the line.

Short managed to enter into a conversation with Courtright
and promised there'd be no gunplay on his part, but he did not
keep his word. Under the guise of searching his vest pocket, he beat
Courtright to the draw and shot him dead in the street. For the first
and last time, Courtright came in second best in a gun battle.

He died on the wrong side of the law, but he had also earned
the reputation of peace officer, scout, and good soldier.

Longhair Jim Courtright left Iowa and his "Gone to Texas"
notation when but a lad, but he died a full-grown man in a dusty
Fort Worth street.

The Democratic Way

Discouraging words were heard, deer and antelope refused to play, and the skies were cloudy all day. It was March 31, 1883, and the cowboys walked off the job.

Until that time, the cowboy had been famed for his loyalty and fierce dedication to the outfit he'd hired out to. His work ethic was the stuff of legend and song. Hard work, long hours, and bad groceries had been stoically endured back in them good old days, but that streak ended on the last day of March, when the cowhands proclaimed their discontent.

The strike was called by Tom Harris at a gathering in a dugout in old Tascosa, with an attendance of better than three hundred disgruntled cowpokes hunkerin' around a wood-burning stove. (It was a big, big dugout, by the way.)

Fiery speeches were orated, and accumulated gripes were many and varied. Around the middle of the morning, a call for a show of hands was requested to show whether the cowboys were in favor of a strike.

The cowboys wanted more money and were honest and adamant enough to say so. Besides just ordinary, everyday swearing, they recited the "Pauper's Oath" and vowed that they'd no longer turn a hand for a measly thirty bucks per month, which was the going rate in that day and time. Nossir, by George, they'd demand fifty dollars for hands and seventy-five for ramrods. They felt that a mass exodus would extract those amounts from the tight-fisted ranchers. Additionally, the strikers hinted darkly that scab replacements might fall victim to ill health should they fill the vacated positions. Range fires and fence cutting were other possibilities should the landholders exhibit the effrontery of ignoring the demands.

Alas, a hand count failed to activate a two-thirds majority at that dugout delegation, and Tom Harris, the chairman, was sorely vexed. But he had an ace in the hole and summarily produced it at that juncture. Seth Riley, from the panhandle of Oklahoma, rose and hobbled slowly to the wooden barrel speaker's stand and looked shyly at his audience of cowhands. Several in the crowd knew Seth, and they howdied him by name and helped to ease his nervousness.

He began by telling them how he had begun cowboying when he was a lad of sixteen years. In 1850, he had hired out to the Charles Goodnight operation up near the top end of Texas; there, he stated, he had enjoyed fair treatment, good food, and sufficient money to support himself. He was single at the time and did not require a lot of money to get by.

His normal job when on a cattle drive or moving a herd to a far pasture was as "night hawk." He rode the outside edge of the stock once they were bunched up for the night.

One dark and moonless night, Seth was slouched in his saddle and meandering slowly around the herd, when "all hell broke loose." The sound of wagon wheels on rocky outcroppings was accompanied by an ear-shattering din of banging and clattering. The lead steer aroused, showed the whites of his fear-filled eyes, and the remainder of the herd did likewise. In an instant, they were stampeding hell for leather away from the alarming sounds.

Seth tried his best to turn them and make them run in a circle, but his mount stepped into a prairie dog hole and snapped his left front leg like a matchstick. Seth and his horse were trampled by the raging herd, and Seth almost died from internal injuries and broken bones. His horse had to be terminated.

He was transported back to his home in Oklahoma as soon as he was able to travel, and the doctors agreed that Seth's cowboy career was at an end. He was told by the ranch foreman that his employment on the Goodnight spread was over with. He did not

receive any money, nor did he get any contribution from his employer to help with the medical expenses. His line of work during his slow healing was as a "hand for hire" in Amarillo.

"I don't think they done me right." He added ruefully. "They could have at least said 'Much obliged, go to hell' or something. I've never heard a word until this day."

The assemblage was sympathetic and also curious to learn what had been the source of all the noise that caused the stampede. "It was a contraption that Mr. Goodnight designed and built," Seth explained. "It was most likely the first one ever made. It was a cook wagon with pots, pans, and all the rigging necessary to keep the hands fed.

"They'd just finished it up that day and wanted to sneak it into camp in the dark of the moon and surprise us at sunup, but they made one mistake when they hung the pans too close to one another. The second mistake was when the cook drove the wagon through that patch of rocky ground. That infernal noise spooked the herd, and they run across me and ruint me for life when my pony broke his leg."

There was total silence throughout the dugout as Seth limped his way through the crowd and left the meeting.

"Back then, they called the Goodnight invention Chuck's wagon, since his hands called him Chuck when he was not around. Today the vehicle is a common sight and is known as the chuck wagon," Tom added.

"Is that story the Gospel truth?" someone in back asked.

"*¿Quien sabe?*" Tom answered. "Now let's have another show of hands on this here strike we've been talking about."

Every hand in the audience was raised, and the first cowboy strike of all time was the unanimous will of the three hundred ranch hands who walked off the job.

There was a strike fund, of course, and each cowboy was offered thirty days of room and board in metropolitan Tascosa, while negotiations were being conducted with the ranch owners.

A wonderful time was had by them strikers. They slept well, ate good, and enjoyed all the head-cracker gin they could put down. The negotiators joined the party, and before you knowed it, the entire fund was gone. And so was the fun.

Meantime, the ranch owners hired drifters and ribbon clerks, and the cattle raising operation went right along. It turned out that they were lots of men who were able and willing to work for thirty greenbacks a month. They liked the money, a place to sleep, and the fare of fatback and pinto beans set well in their bellies.

Busted and hung over, the strikers got back into the job-hunting line, but they found mighty cool receptions at their former places of employment.

"You left me in a bind," one rancher told a former hand, "and I can't use you no more. As far as I'm concerned, you're a free agent."

Tom Landry, longtime coach of the Dallas chapter of Cowboys, would use a similar line in times to come.

Catalostrophic

A blue norther blew in on the first day of February in 1899, and before it ran out of wind four days later, it rated a close second to the Ice Age. Entering Texas up in the Dalhart and Tulia country, it buried every strand of barbed wire in the storied fence that acts as the buffer zone between Texas and the North Pole.

In addition to a shortage of stove wood and hazardous trips to the outhouse, that cold snap also played havoc with Mary Anne Goodnight's herd of catalos by a most unusual circumstance. Her famous husband, Colonel Charles, admitted that he'd never seen anything to beat it.

Mary was foolish about the buffalo, and in the beginning she had a two-mile square of land to accommodate her hobby zoo. Back in '79, Colonel Charles roped two orphan calves as antes for Mary's pleasure. She bottle-fed them at a rate of three gallons per day until they got their legs under them and switched to solid food.

From that point, they practiced their uncanny ability to unstring fences and parade around the Panhandle festooned with halos of barbed wire. This distressed Mary and really got Colonel Charles's hackles up. It was so disturbing to him that he slew them bisons, and he and Mary wintered on jerked buffalo.

THE LEGACY

A couple of years later the colonel, who was a crackerjack innovator, took the notion to cross-breed his shorthorn cattle with the grizzled buffalo. Unabashed cooperation from both species occurred, and he wound up with a sizable herd of what he chose to call "cataloes." Shaggy-haired and with the hump of the buffalo, the progeny had little ambition for fence wrecking, so the colonel was well pleased with his creation.

"A fitting memorial and legacy from a thinking man," he may have said as he placekicked a dry catalo chip through and above the corral gateposts.

The catalo drew scorn from both the shorthorn and the pure stock of buffalo, but the offspring seemed not to care and went about their dining and procreating with great industry.

Now, when that granddaddy of blizzards blindsided the Texas Panhandle on February 1, the thermometers all froze up and busted, and tragedy was close behind. Colonel Charles and Anne witnessed the demise of their catalo herd with consternation and disbelief.

Most everyone knows that cattle turn their back ends to a norther, but not the shaggy old buffalo. With that dense growth of hair on his head and shoulders, he opts to face the worst Mother Nature can deal out. The only concession the buffalo will make is a slight squint of his eyes if the breeze kicks up above seventy miles per hour.

These diametrically opposing genetic traits were the undoing of the catalo. They exhausted themselves swapping ends and finally, in desperation, they turned broadside to the Mother of All Texas Blizzards.

Naturally, they all froze.

Look! Up in the Sky!

Aurora, Wise Co., Tex., April 17—About 2 o'clock this morning the early risers of Aurora were astonished at the sudden appearance of the airship which has been sailing through the country. It was traveling due north, and much nearer the earth than ever before. Evidently some of the machinery was out of order, for it was making a speed of only ten or twelve miles an hour and gradually settling toward the earth. It sailed directly over the public square, and when it reached the north part of town, collided with the tower of Judge Proctor's windmill and went to pieces with a terrific explosion, scattering debris over several acres, wrecking the windmill and water tank and destroying the judge's flower garden.

T. J. Weems, the U.S. Signal Service officer at this place and authority on astronomy, gives it as his opinion that he [the pilot] was a native of the planet Mars.

Papers found on his person—evidently the record of his travels—are written in some unknown hieroglyphics and cannot be deciphered.

The ship was too badly wrecked to form any conclusion as to its construction or motive power. It was built of some unknown metal, resembling somewhat a mixture of aluminum and silver."
(from an old newspaper clipping)

That amazing revelation was published in the *Dallas Morning News* on April 19, 1887, and the writer credited was a Mr. S. E. Haydon. No other Texas publication picked up on the startling expose, but one publisher up in Wichita Falls opined that the article ran "eighteen days late." One nationally respected magazine, *Harper's Weekly,* saw fit to publish data on the rare sightings in three consecutive editions. Accounts had been reported in Illinois, Wisconsin, and Iowa before the airship put in an appearance in the skies over Denton, and that was only the debut. Rapid-fire reports of a cigar-shaped aircraft, ablaze with excess lighting, were reported at Weatherford, Corsicana, Stephenville, and Fort Worth, where the craft actually alighted in the city park. Blazing speed was definitely established when, that same day, it was spotted over Denver, Colorado, and was accorded mention in the *Rocky Mountain News.*

Now, to help get a handle on this matter it must be stated that six years would come and go before the Wright boys managed to get their flying contraption off the ground up at Kitty Hawk, North Carolina. The acronym "UFO" had not been coined, so the strange apparition was described as "the damndest sight you'll ever see."

Graveside services were conducted at the Aurora Cemetery, and a stone marker was set. The Greek letter delta was the extent of the engraving, and there are citizens of Aurora still alive who recall the marker. Unfortunately, it was either stolen or beamed up when nobody was around, so it cannot be introduced into evidence at this time.

The incident was mostly forgotten until 1973, when UFO fever was at fever pitch, and Aurora was back in the news with its "Close Encounters" legend.

Major General Donald E. Keyhoe, who was head man of the National Investigative Committee on Aerial Phenomena of Quincy, Illinois, and lauded as America's foremost authority on terrestrial comings and goings, hied himself down to Texas for in-depth interviews and on-the-ground investigation.

He was handicapped by the fact that all the eyewitnesses to the 1897 catastrophe had gone on to their eternal rewards. The only testimony available was from descendents and their recall of tales their parents had told them. It turned out that S. E. Haydon, who reported the incident to the *Dallas Morning News,* never existed. Mr. F. E. Hayden, an area cotton buyer, is suspected as the probable writer, and he was probably trying to drum up a little business for Aurora.

Additionally, there was never a Judge Proctor who lost a windmill in the terrible crash, if there was one, and F. E. Hayden was not mayor of Aurora. He was a justice of the peace, and that is several links below judge on the food chain.

T. J. Weems may have lacked credentials and expertise in his diagnosis of Mars as home base for the spacecraft and occupants. Old T. J. owned and operated a blacksmith shop, and the heat from his forge may have had adverse effects on his thinking.

Scrupulous investigation did yield shards of an unidentifiable metal scattered over a wide area where the accident is reputed to have occurred, but they are not shards from a windmill. To top that off, to this day no vegetation will grow upon the impact area, which was the site of Proctor's garden.

The cigar-shaped spacecraft apparently sterilized that plot of ground forevermore, according to UFO experts from Yankee Country.

Just another fine example of the harm that tobacco or cigar-shaped UFOs can wreak upon human and plant life.

Hell's Half-Acre

Hell's Half-Acre flourished in Fort Worth from around 1874 until its passing was announced in late 1889. Reports of its death, like Mark Twain's, was greatly exaggerated, however. Activity was more discreet and muted, but Hell's Half-Acre was still in operation until the onset of the roaring twenties, and thereafter, as some will tell you.

Geographically, the Acre centered on today's Commerce and 12th Street, and every once in a while the half-acre designation ballooned to encompass somewhere between two and three acres.

As early as March 1874, three hundred fistfights were reported on a single Saturday night, and it was only an average night in Hell's Half-Acre. At that time, the population of Fort Worth was but 2,200, and figuring that the female population was about the same number as the men and then allowing a third of the citizens to be children, one can cipher the approximate number of adult males in the head count to be around seven hundred. Therefore, 350 man-to-man bouts are about the elastic limit of native-son tiffs that could be arranged with the available male population. To maintain that tempo, outside brawlers were necessary. Cattle drovers, cowboys, and rural types provided the sustaining force to keep the entertainment area functioning at full steam.

Three-dollar fines for public drunkenness hurt business for the gaming establishments as well as for the painted damsels who kept rooms at the various bed-and-breakfast emporiums. The fine was lowered to the affordable fee of one dollar in 1878, and unlike Enron, the bars and sporting houses made a complete financial recovery.

That change in July resulted in a reported count of twenty-five ladies actively plying their trade at the Red Light Dine and Dance in the month of December. And the Red Light was not the only firm engaged in the tourist trade.

A seesaw battle between good and evil ensued. Joints were closed, bars were fined, and the feminine population waned and waxed. But despite the most honorable intentions of Mayor Beckham's vow to enforce ordinances and civilize the wild ones, the show went on. And on.

In 1887 yet another reforming mayor, Mr. H. S. Broiles, inaugurated another crackdown on the behavior in Hell's Half-Acre. He banned the sale of liquor on the Sabbath.

Former Mayor Beckham had advanced to district judge status, and his years of experience and his clout in inflicting sizable fines upon the revelers took such a bite out of the financial rewards of the entertainment trade that Hell's Half-Acre boarded up the bordellos, poured the surplus intoxicants in the Trinity River, and went into church construction. Peace and quiet had replaced the high old times in Hell's Half-Acre by the time 1900 heralded the beginning of a brave new century.

If you believe that, you never visited the Bomber Grill or the Brass Rail in downtown Fort Worth during the years that featured World War II, and it's possible that pockets of similar activities survive in this century.

Rakin' It In

Crazy Ben Sublett showed up at the only saloon in Odessa sometime in 1891. He had empty pockets, was considered loco, and had no luck at all in mooching a drink in that high-class establishment. As a matter of fact, he was instructed by the bartender to pursue his panhandling at another location.

From that point, his reputation around Ector County waned. To a point.

Wandering around in the wilds of western Texas was considered to be a chancy occupation in those days, due to the hostile Indians who lurked in wait for the unwary. Crazy Ben, by virtue of his "insane" diagnoses, wandered freely, due to the belief of the Native Americans that the Great Spirit took a dim view of anyone bringing harm to an idiot. That afflicted sort was considered to be a creature of the Great Manitou.

Time passed, and Ben was seldom seen around town until the day he walked through the saloon batwings with a half-filled tow sack on his shoulder. Before he could be ordered to leave or be thrown out, Ben poured a sampling of the contents of his sack onto the bar. It was wire gold and solid nuggets, and the dimly lighted bar lit up like the Milky Way. Ben's acceptance into the saloon and the upper crust of Odessa society was instantaneous and semi-sincere. He was saturated with free liquor and surrounded by friends in a heartbeat.

"Where in tarnation did you get all that gold?" was the first question Ben fielded after he'd irrigated his whistle.

"Out yonder in the Guadalupes," he said.

"Where abouts?"

"I may be crazy," Ben responded, "but I ain't stupid! The Guadalupes is west of here. 'Bout halfway to El Paso as I calculate, and them are about the only directions I'm willing to share with you. If you were not my friend I wouldn't a told you that much! I didn't need a shovel to get it neither—I use a rake."

Ben marketed his gold over in Midland and appeared spasmodically, when he was low on funds, until his death just prior to the turn of the century.

Experienced trackers tried in vain to follow Ben to his treasure trove, but he always made his journey in the dark of the moon and at unpredictable times.

He did not leave a map, and to this day no one else has stumbled onto Ben's bonanza. But they did find some oil in that country.

One-Eyed Eagle

Wile E. Coyote trades with Acme to facilitate his ongoing ambition to catch a roadrunner, but Wiley Post of Grand Saline struck a deal with Goodrich when he needed an article for his chosen line of work. A little farther down the road, the historic incident will be revealed.

Wiley Post was born in Grand Saline, Texas, on November 22, 1898, and he had almost as much salt in him as the ground below. He carried it with him when his folks moved to Oklahoma in 1909 and settled near the oil fields of Lawton.

In his seventeenth year, he went to work in those oil fields and developed a love and fascination for things mechanical; his teenagery beguiled him into stealing a car in 1921. He was proven guilty, convicted, and sentenced to ten years in the penitentiary. He was granted a parole after one year and had learned his lesson. He steered clear of any further brushes with the law.

An oilfield accident took his left eye, but instead of cursing the darkness, Wiley Post chose to light a candle. He used his $1,800 settlement to purchase an airplane, which he learned to fly.

Fate brought Wiley and Will Rogers together in 1925, when Will was running late for an appearance at a rodeo. Wiley got him there on time, and a friendship was forged.

Mostly by reputation, Wiley hired on with a wealthy oilman, F. C. Hall, and was entrusted with the use of Hall's open-cockpit biplane. Shortly thereafter, Hall bought a Lockheed Vega, which he called *Winnie Mae* to honor his daughter. Wiley, of course, stayed on as Mr. Hall's private pilot, but hard times accompanied by the national depression forced Hall out of the airplane business.

When 1930 rolled around, Hall purchased a later model of the Lockheed Vega, and it too wore Winnie Mae's name. It was the hottest model of its type in the sky, and Wiley Post was at the controls. Its maximum speed was 170 mph, and it would cruise at 140 and had a range of 725 miles. It went for a little better than eighteen thousand dollars. It earned a reputation as one of the most famous mechanical birds in the blue and set many records. *Winnie Mae,* along with about 130 carbon copies, was designed by John Northrupt and Gerrard Vultee, each of whom later went on to own their own aircraft companies.

Wiley Post had a female counterpart who also flew the Lockheed Vega. Her name was Amelia Earhart.

In 1931, Wiley piloted the *Winnie Mae* around the world in eight days. His navigator on the flight was Harold Gatty, who later served on General Douglas MacArthur's staff.

Wiley and Harold departed Roosevelt Field in New York on June 23, 1931. In all they made fourteen stops on their globe-circling flight. They set down back at New York on July 1, having logged 15,474 miles.

Their trip was not accomplished without problems. Two inches of water covered an airfield in Siberia, and the plane sank into the mud. It took fourteen hours to wrestle the *Winnie Mae* from the mire, and an even more serious dilemma befell them in Solomon, Alaska.

With a full tank of fuel, Wiley was taxiing along a beach for takeoff when the *Winnie Mae* sank into the sand and bent both tips of the prop. Wiley beat it back into a shape with a rusty hammer and a rock, and that got the craft back into the air. The damaged propeller was replaced at their next stop, Fairbanks, Alaska. Arriving without further complications, they lunched at the White House and were treated to a ticker-tape parade on July 6.

Wiley wound up owning the *Winnie Mae* and installed some new fangled autopilot and navigation apparatus, encored the round-the-world flight solo, and hacked twenty-one hours from his own record circumnavigation by setting down in seven days and nineteen hours.

Wiley then turned his attention to high-altitude, long-distance flights. Since the *Winnie Mae*'s cabin could not be pressurized, he collaborated with Goodrich Rubber and fabricated the first pressure suit, which led to development of the outfits now worn by the explorers of space. Goodrich served Wiley Post much better than Acme has done by Wile E. Coyote.

Post soared to new heights with his innovative equipment, reaching unheard of altitudes of fifty-thousand-plus and locating the jet stream in the process. In 1935, utilizing the jet stream, he flew his 179 mph plane from California to Cleveland, Ohio, in a few minutes better than seven hours, averaging a ground speed of almost 200 mph, pioneering pressurized flight as we know it today.

Wiley retired *Winnie Mae* and turned to designing a plane capable of making a mail run from the West Coast to Russia. He combined parts of two Lockheed airplanes, installed a Wasp motor and larger fuel tanks, and affixed pontoons to facilitate landing on water. Its unusual configuration prompted wags to call the craft "Wiley's Bastard," but his old buddy Will Rogers referred to it as the "Aurora Borealis" and elected to go along with Wiley on a shakedown flight up Alaska way.

Bad weather forced them down near Point Barrow to gather information on their location, and the engine malfunctioned when they tried to take off. Both men were killed instantly in that shallow lagoon within twenty miles of their destination.

The *Winnie Mae* was sold to the Smithsonian Museum by Wiley's widow.

A Texas-born, one-eyed eagle blazed the trail that led to the exploration of space.

Packing Heat

It was a miserably hot July in 1898, and the merchants of Corsicana were eager for a gimmick to lure customers from their front porches into town. A one-legged tightrope walker was passing through Corsicana, and he fired the imagination of those business operators with accounts of his rope-walking ability.

Feeling that such an attraction would surely entice folks to come downtown, the merchants came to terms with the talented performer, an agreement was struck, and the event was scheduled for July 28.

Someone noticed that the rope walker's peg leg was grooved to receive the rope, and many announced disappointment at such an advantage. The aerialist smilingly volunteered to strap a cast iron stove to his back to offset the advantage, and the merchants agreed that such an added attraction was more than fair.

On the appointed day, a tightrope was stretched across Beaton Street between business houses. The band played, the crowd gathered, and at the appointed hour, the rope walker appeared atop one of the buildings to which his wire was anchored. The stove was indeed strapped onto his back, and as he positioned himself for his walk, a hush fell upon the gathered town folk.

To his credit, he was performing the walk admirably, but somewhere near midspan the rope began to stretch due to the added weight of the stove. Unable to maintain his balance on the oscillating rope, he fell to the street, completely destroying the stove and inflicting a sizable dent in the pavement.

Before he died, he said he was from Princeton, New Jersey, and that his birth date was February 6, 1829. If he gave his name no one caught it.

This lamentable turn of events did not stay a decent burial and a headstone in Corsicana's Hebrew Cemetery.

The headstone has but two engraved words: "Rope Walker."

No Beef from Joe Loving

Two hundred fifty-three counties had been organized in Texas when the surveyors and land planners noticed they'd overlooked an irregular tract east of the southern New Mexico line and the Pecos River. They studied the matter over, naturally, and did what needed to be done.

Long before the Civil War, Texas teemed with long-horned cattle, which were correctly referred to as "jerky on the hoof." They were descendents of the Spanish cattle that had been abandoned or escaped during the time Spain laid claim to Mexico and Texas.

Those wiry specimens were fleet of foot, with wolf deterrents of prodigious dimension mounted on both sides of their heads. They holed up in mesquite thickets during the day and did most of their foraging by the light of the moon. They were the ultimate survivors and could sustain life on pastures that wouldn't feed a goat.

When the Civil War played out, Charles Goodnight saw dollar signs on the free-ranging swarms of longhorns. He also knew that there were railheads at Dodge City and Abilene, Kansas. A railroad could transport cattle into the waiting markets of the East if a man could manage to herd a payload from Texas to Kansas. But he also knew that a ready market for beef existed a little closer to home. Government agencies needed meat to feed the concentration of Indians over in New Mexico. He also knew that the wild cattle abounded in the Palo Pinto country, and that was sufficient data to inspire him to take the gamble and travel the shorter distance.

There were problems to be solved. He needed a competent and able-bodied man to help him get safely across ninety miles of the Llano Estacado. He began his search for just the right man and found slim pickings until he ran across Joe Loving.

Joe was the most experienced cattle drover in Texas and had been the very first man to trail a herd across the state line. Goodnight stated his plan honestly to Joe Loving.

They discussed the bands of renegade Comanches who roved the Staked Plains and the lack of water and grass.

"I'm willing to chance it," Goodnight said, "and I'd like you to go with me." Joe listened with keen interest and then considered the chances of failure against the rewards of pulling it off.

"When are we leaving?" He finally asked.

In the spring of 1867, the two managed to put together a herd of four thousand head and bunched them near the headwaters of the Concho River. They spent a few days to allow the herd to eat, drink, and get in traveling shape.

The days passed, the trail crew reported, and the herd strung out and headed due west toward Horsehead Crossing on the Pecos River, ninety-six miles distant.

They did not pause for three days and four nights. The days were torrid, the nights were chilly, and the disturbed dust could be seen for miles. The cattle were weary, hungry, thirsty, and had to be prodded to keep the pace.

When they were within a few miles of the Pecos, the lead steer lifted his head and sniffed out the water; the whole herd perked up and required no more urging to reach the river. Charles and Joe felt that they'd completed the most difficult leg of the drive.

Water, forage, and three days of rest restored the spirits and stamina of man and beast, and the drive resumed up the shallow valley of the Pecos.

Comanches harassed the drovers, stealing a few head of cattle and causing jittery nerves in the men. By the middle of June, the herd was about a hundred miles north of Horsehead Crossing, and an appearance at Fort Sumner by a representative of the herd was mandatory by the beginning of July to ensure fulfillment of the contract.

Joe Loving volunteered to get to the fort and took Bill Wilson along with him. It was a chancy ride for two men, and Goodnight cautioned them to travel in the dark of night and hole up in the brush during daylight hours.

"It's the only safe way to travel in Comanche country," Goodnight said. Joe and Bill agreed and struck out for Fort Sumner.

They stayed with the plan for the first two nights, but Joe didn't like the night riding, and at dawn of the third day he convinced Bill that they could make better time by switching to daylight travel.

"Not as likely to have one of the horses break a leg in a prairie dog hole, and we'll have more luck at sleeping if we do it at night when it ain't so blamed hot." Joe was eager to agree, and since they'd seen no sign of Indians, he was willing to go along with the new strategy.

Near the middle of that afternoon they spotted a war party, and at the same time the party caught sight of Joe and Bill. They made a run for cover and managed to reach a high bank of the Pecos. They descended the sandy hundred-foot drop off, crossed the river, and found cover in a dense cane break.

An exchange of gunfire erupted, but the drovers had the edge, since they had repeating rifles and plenty of ammunition. They held the Comanches at bay until the coming of darkness, but Joe took bullets in the arm and side. He was not in any shape to ride, and he convinced Bill to make his escape and make a try at getting back to the herd.

Bill refused at first, but Joe insisted that nothing was to be gained by the death of both. Just before dawn, Bill eased into the slow-moving waters of the Pecos and quietly drifted through the circle of Comanches.

He left the rifle and several six-guns with Joe. Once safely downriver, he climbed the bank and headed back to the herd on foot. He was near naked and barefooted.

Three days later he stumbled into camp, totally exhausted and fevered. Goodnight took a dozen of his best men and rode immediately in search of Joe Loving. They found the battle site, but they did not find Joe. They assumed that he had been killed and thrown into the Pecos River. A downriver search was considered to be a futile effort, so they returned to the herd. They still had to get the beef to Fort Sumner.

They were met a few days later by a search party out of the fort and were stunned to learn that Joe had managed to escape by the same method as Bill. He had lain in the weeds all the next day, and the Indians went away after a less than thorough search.

Night came and Joe had staggered and crawled along a trail that he believed to lead to Fort Sumner. He had gone until he could not muster the strength to go farther and collapsed due to weakness from blood loss. After five days, Mexican riders found him and carried him to the fort.

Goodnight and Bill hurried straightway to the fort and found Joe still alive but with a badly infected arm. The doctor assured them that Joe didn't have a chance unless that arm was amputated immediately. With no other option, the operation was done, but Joe died from shock and loss of blood on September 25, 1867.

"He was a game one," Charles Goodnight stated, and that epitaph was fitting accolade for cattle drover Joe Loving.

Loving County, which may or may not have been named in his honor, was the last Texas county to be organized, in 1931.

If this account is vaguely familiar to you, it's possible that you read Larry McMurtry's novel *Lonesome Dove* or saw the movie. They were both well done.

The Maverick President

Theodore "Teddy" Roosevelt was president of the United States back in 1904, and he got the job as a wildcard entry in the sweepstakes for head honcho up at Washington on the Potomac.

He was rough cut and adventuresome in his lifetime, and unusual feats held a mighty attraction for him. That's why he accepted the invitation to attend an out-of-the-dotted-line contest up around Wichita Falls in the mesquite thickets.

W. T. Waggoner and a rancher buddy, S. Burk Burnett, with help and advice from Colonel Cecil Lyon, invited Teddy to come down to Texas and behold Jack Abernathy's expertise at catching wolves and coyotes with his bare hands and a fast horse. It must have seemed bully entertainment to the president, since he showed up.

At that time, a big part of Oklahoma, just north of the Red River, was known as the "big pasture." That vast acreage was set aside as open range. It was unfenced and offered grazing for anyone who owned a hungry cow. It also teemed with jackass rabbits and their natural predators, wolves and coyotes.

Jack Abernathy, an Oklahoma rancher, was famed for his ability to overtake a coyote or wolf, muzzle it, hogtie it, and take it back for the admiration of the spectators. Jack was successful on his first attempt, and President Teddy was amazed and delighted with the performance. The speed and agility of Jack Abernathy's mount was praised by President Roosevelt and his party.

W. T. Waggoner owned a fair-sized ranch, and he stated that he too had ponies that could outrun and outmaneuver a coyote.

As proof, he summoned Bony Moore of Electra and requested that he mount "Doggie" and bring in another coyote. Bony, a hand on the Waggoner spread, was overjoyed at the opportunity. He and Doggie exhausted a coyote and brought it back to camp all trussed up, and Doggie was not even breathing hard. Texas honor was maintained, and Oklahoma graciously agreed to share bragging rights to coyote capturing by "the bare hand method."

The unusual outing got a lot of ink back on the East Coast, and naturally Teddy drew a little heat for the way he spent his leisure hours. He apparently did not take much notice or even care.

As a matter of fact, he invited Bony and the wife up to the Christmas Party at the White House in 1905.

Emigrant Legend

There are many in this old world of ours who hold that things break about even for all of us. I have observed, for example, that we all get about the same amount of ice. The rich get it in the summertime and the poor get it in the winter."

The author of those words died at his desk October 25, 1921, and that observation was written on a pad that was found beside his still body. That parting shot may have been a future topic or a cynical observation on life.

William came to Texas as a boy in the early 1800s. His homeport, until that time, was the state of Illinois, but once in Texas William apprenticed out as a buffalo hunter in western Texas. He mastered the trade under the tutelage of Billy Dixon, who was a seasoned scout, frontiersman, and buffalo hunter.

The killing and skinning of the numberless herds of buffalo was a profitable enterprise in that day and time, but the Kiowas, Cheyennes, and Comanche Indians frowned on the practice and decided that the white man had overstayed his welcome. They assembled into a war party and trailed a party of the buffalo killers to a point in present-day Hutchison County between Bent and Adobe Creeks and the South Canadian River in the panhandle of Texas. The three sod buildings at that location were known as Adobe Walls. Two of them were grocery stores, the third was a saloon, and the settlement was a market place and pickup point for the buffalo hide trade. A few days off and laying in provisions were

necessary once in a while for the buffalo-killing crews. The liquor was passable too, should a man desire to wet his whistle. Most did. Slaughtering and skinning buffalo was not a trade for ribbon clerks. William and those he worked with were at Adobe Walls on June 27, 1874, when Indian forces attacked at dawn, with the rising sun at their backs. Their leader was Quanah Parker, the fierce half-breed, blue-eyed chief of the Comanches.

Billy Dixon was first to see the onrushing Indians and fired the first shot, but the distance was too great to score a hit. He made a wild dash for Hanrahan's Saloon, and the other hunters were alerted and quickly positioned themselves with their "Big Fifty" buffalo guns of the Sharps and Winchester varieties.

The coalition of braves from the plains tribes were mounted on their finest steeds and resplendent in their war paint. For protection, they wielded multi-ply buffalo-hide shields, and scalps of previous forays were décor for the horses' bridles. With war bonnets of colored feathers and their guns at ready, the warrior cream of the tribes came charging at full speed directly into the street separating the three business houses.

The shrieking Indians were greeted with volleys of massive slugs from the rifles of the hide hunters. There were members of the group in all three buildings, and the rifle barrels were extended through gun slits, catching the braves in a murderous crossfire. Both riders and their mounts were felled by the score.

The Indians dismounted. Some reached the heavy door and tried to break through with their rifle butts, but their knock was answered with fire from six-guns.

From his vantage point, Chief Parker saw that the war was going in favor of the hide hunters, so he called his braves into retreat.

Three days came and went, and the dead and wounded increased with each charge. The sharp-shooting buffalo hunters detracted from the braves' number on each occasion of an assault. William and Bill stood shoulder to shoulder at slits in the saloon wall, and very little of their ammunition went to waste. Stone Calf, son of the Cheyenne chief, was one of the fatalities, and his loss hastened a loss of heart for the Indian force.

The third day broke their spirits completely. Billy Dixon fired his big Sharps at a brave sitting his pony around forty-five hundred feet away, and that shot really took the starch out of the Indians. They turned their horses and retreated from Adobe Walls.

A tally of Indian losses could not be made, since most of the dead and wounded were removed from the battlefield, but the remaining corpses numbered twelve, and there were over fifty dead horses.

Four of the buffalo hunters died—three from Indian fire and one by an accidental discharge of his own weapon. That man was Bill Olds, and his wife was the only white woman in the defense of Adobe Walls. Twenty-year-old William came through unmarked but battle tempered. He did not pursue the waning herds of buffalo for very long after that historic battle. Twenty-six hide hunters had held an army of the cream of plains Indians at bay for three days with only four fatalities.

William signed on with General Nelson Miles's Indian-

COMANCHE GOLD

chasing cavalry for a brief period of time, but the yen to see different country sent him adrift, and he wound up in Dodge City, Kansas.

The coming of the Santa Fe Railroad had changed Dodge City from a sleepy crossroads village into a hellhole teeming with gamblers, outlaws, cowboys, and buffalo hunters. Feminine affection was also available if a man had money in his pocket.

Will hired on as a peace officer; he advanced to deputy sheriff and then was elected sheriff of Dodge City. He spent two years in Dodge and earned the respect of all when David Rudabaugh's gang robbed a train at Kinsley, Kansas. Kinsley lay well outside William's territory of authority, but he was not deterred by a trivial detail like that. William gathered a posse and, despite a raging snowstorm, beat the Rudabaugh gang to a cow camp that was suspected to be their hideout.

William and the deputized posse members arrived to find the place deserted, so they patiently waited with loaded rifles, and sure enough, their patience was rewarded. The robber band, half-frozen, surrendered without a fight

With his Texas background and acquaintances, Will then focused his attention on the rowdy Texas cowhands who liked to whoop it up in Dodge City after completion of their drives. He was able to convince those Yankee-despising Texans to check their sidearms and weapons before they enjoyed the festivities. Without gunplay or overt force he managed to enforce the new rule, and a good time was still enjoyed by the Texan visitors.

The single incident that brought out the killer instinct in William occurred in 1878. His brother Ed was serving in the capacity of marshal during a trip to Texas by the appointed marshal—one Wyatt Earp.

Jack Wagner and a crony, Alf Walker, gunned Ed down on Front Street, and brother William hurried to the scene. He killed Wagner with a single shot to the belly and put two rounds through Walker. One bullet struck his right arm and the other passed through a lung. Walker managed to mount his horse, make his getaway, and get back to Texas, only to die of pneumonia from an infection of his lung. When Wyatt returned, he and William tamed Dodge City. By 1879, William had had his fill of Dodge City and of being a peace officer. He opted for a new line of endeavor, so he went to Denver, Colorado, and opened a saloon and gambling mecca. He operated that establishment until 1902 and, being forty-eight years old and little better off financially than when he had arrived in Texas, sold his saloon and ranged back to Texas.

He got lucky in a high-stakes game and at the same time was offered a high-paying job as personal bodyguard to George Gould, a railroad tycoon of New York City.

There, William drew his pay and started an entirely new career. He had always loved boxing, and he got a part-time position on the *Morning Telegraph* staff as a sportswriter. He discovered a natural talent for the newspaper game and eventually rose to the editor's post.

In 1905 President Roosevelt, a man cut from similar cloth, appointed William as U.S. deputy marshal for the district of New York. He served in that capacity for two years, but the newspaper business still beckoned. He responded and performed in a creditable capacity until his death in 1921. He was survived by a wife and children he had accrued in New York.

When his body was discovered lying across his desk October 25, 1921, William Barclay Masterson had done a heap of living in his sixty-seven years, and his philosophy of life may have been encapsulated in that final note.

It was, of course not signed, but if it had been he would probably have signed off with the name by which he was remembered by his many old compadres. He was simply "Bat Masterson."

Woe in Waco

George Bruce Gerald, his wife, and four young children relocated from Mississippi to the bustling little city of Waco, Texas, in 1869. Times were hard in Mississippi, and the Geralds came in search of new scenery, different acquaintances, and a place to put down roots and call home. Waco seemed to fill the bill. An attorney by education, George Gerald hung out his shingle and assumed editorship of the *Examiner,* a thriving weekly newspaper. His credentials qualified him in that pursuit and earned him election to a judgeship in 1870. For Gerald the American dream appeared to be approaching reality.

Details of Judge Gerald's boyhood back in Mississippi were unknown and not shared with the populace of Waco, however. In his youth and law school days in Lebanon, Tennessee, Judge Gerald had been a firebrand with a hair trigger and the grit of an acre of sandpaper. A well-honed knife, bigger than the standard Bowie, was his weapon of choice, and he was well qualified in its use. He did not seek out trouble, but similarly, he did not hide from it.

When the Civil War got under way, he enlisted immediately and was a rough and ready participant. His fierceness earned him rapid advancement through the ranks, and his boldness accrued him four serious wounds. He commanded the Eighteenth Mississippi Infantry Regiment at the battle of Gettysburg, where he almost lost his life. His left arm was shattered, and he lost much of its usefulness for the remainder of his life.

When he assumed editorship of the *Waco Examiner,* George Gerald wielded his pen with the same dexterity he had shown with his knife. Whatever talent he lacked at editorializing was amply compensated for by his directness and honesty in words that could be understood by a child. He called a spade a spade, unless he stumbled over it in the dark.

The *Examiner*'s office was located on the public square in downtown Waco, and William Edmond, a young law clerk, had a desk in the editorial office.

On one occasion a disturbed reader stormed into the office and demanded the attention of the editor. William pointed to Gerald, who was busy at his desk and did not look up at the disturbance or acknowledge the irate, uninvited guest.

The complainant strode angrily across the room and stood straight and grim for a sign of recognition.

Gerald placed his pen delicately upon the desktop, rose and grabbed the intruder's collar with his bad left arm and the top of his pants with the right. Then he propelled the uninvited guest forward and through an open window, which looked out upon the city street. The fact that Gerald's office was on the second floor did not matter to him, but as he returned to his writing, William went to the window to view the probable carnage. Luckily, a large shrub had broken the man's inglorious descent and spared him a broken neck or limb. He had bounced from the shrub and rolled into the dirt street. He arose, dusted himself off, and without a backward glance, departed the area. He was apparently satisfied, since he never again visited the editorial office of the *Examiner.*

Judge Gerald embellished his reputation as a man of action following a heated trial concerning legal ownership of a strip of land along a border of a farm he owned. He won the lawsuit, retained ownership, and following the verdict he confronted the suing party (a man named Dalton) and fixed him with a withering gaze of distaste. Judge Gerald drew a razor-sharp knife from his pocket and seized Dalton's long, flowing beard in one hand. Then with one swipe he severed the beard from the chin down, tossed it on the courthouse steps, and strode away. Dalton did not follow.

As part of his platform when he was campaigning for a judge-ship, Gerald had pledged the closing of gambling establishments in the city of Waco, and he was a man of his word. He ordered the county sheriff to close the doors of the gaming joints, but the sheriff showed hesitance in the matter, until finally Judge Gerald's patience ran out.

At first light one fine day, the judge strapped on his gun belt and made a beeline to Mr. George Crippen's second-story gaming emporium. It was the most famous of Waco's gambling establishments.

The door was securely locked, but the judge kicked it off its hinges, went inside, and smashed every stick of furniture and tossed it and all the gaming equipment through the window and into the alley.

He then proceeded directly to the offices of the daily newspaper and reported his actions. He requested its publication that very day and added a promise that like treatment would be accorded any and all places of gambling henceforth and forevermore. They took him at his word, and gambling was not in open operation after the incident.

About the same time Judge Gerald made his debut appearance at Waco, a thirteen-year-old lad, William Cowper Brann of Coles County, Illinois, put his few belongings in a sack and crawled out the window of his foster parents' home. He was in the third grade and was desperate to find a better way.

Following his mother's death, he had been placed in the care of a farm couple, William and Mary Hawkins. After nine years on that farm, he took charge of his destiny, and although his formal education was never resumed, he accomplished some remarkable things.

He was employed as a hotel bellboy, a house painter, and eventually as cub reporter on a small Illinois newspaper. At the age of twenty-two, William Cowper Brann married Carrie Belle Martin in Rochelle, Illinois. The young couple drifted to St. Louis, then to Galveston, and on to San Antonio. William plied himself with self-education and earned a deserved reputation as a gifted journalist and editorialist.

After a move to Austin in 1891, William worked for the *Austin Statesman* for a short time, then he gambled his modest bankroll on a small publication of his own. He published the *Iconoclast*

chupp '02

until his money was gone, and then he left Texas, selling his press to William Sydney Porter, who would later achieve fame as O. Henry.

Back once more to Texas, Brann served as editor for the *San Antonio Express* and after a brief stint moved to Houston as chief editorial writer for the *Post*. In 1894, he relocated his family for the final time and hired on as chief editorialist for the *Daily News* in Waco. During his time at that position, he met Judge Gerald, and each recognized a kindred spirit. They became very good friends.

In February 1895, Brann revived the *Iconoclast*, and this time it did not fail, soaring to a circulation of better than a hundred thousand. Brann targeted Baptists, British, and women, revealing his nature as a racist. With glee he assailed Baylor University, its faculty, students, and sympathizers. He referred regularly to Baylor as "the great storm center of misinformation."

Brann's style was venomous and shocking humor, and his self-education and writing style elevated him, in the estimation of many, to the stature of Ambrose Bierce and Mark Twain. The citizenry of Waco, however, confessed a devout dislike for Brann and a distaste for his style of belittlement; within three years, the opposition forces reached epidemic proportions. But they all read his paper. The *Iconoclast* circulation reached out globally, and not everyone condemned Brann for his effrontery in his criticism of his fellow townspeople, who dwelt in the stronghold of Baptist Territory.

Judge Gerald, a member of the freethinkers' movement and a confessed deist, admired Brann's assault of narrow thinking and was a staunch friend and supporter. He took the same view, especially, of the many faults Brann proclaimed in the morals of the female students, and the lamentable lack of intelligence in the entire faculty of Baylor University.

The *Waco Herald* was the latest newspaper in town, and Judge Gerald penned a letter praising Brann and reminding the readers of freedom of the press and the constitutional right to have differing opinions—even in the Bible Belt of Texas—where Baylor University was the belt buckle.

J. W. Harris was owner/operator of the *Times-Herald,* but in addition he was a card-carrying member of the Baptist Church. He refused to run the judge's letter, refused to give a reason, and refused to return the letter. The judge's patience wore thin, and he made a personal call on Harris in the matter.

A fight erupted between the two men in Harris's office, and Harris got in the first blow. As he staggered back, the judge drew his pistol. But Harris reacted quickly and knocked the gun from the judge's hand and shoved him down the stairway and onto the sidewalk. Judge Gerald regained his feet and his dignity and departed the scene, but he did not suffer in silence. The very next day a handbill was distributed on the streets of Waco reporting the incident, accusing Harris of being a liar, a scoundrel, and a coward. As a solution, the judge issued an invitation for Harris to face him in a duel to the death with shotgun, pistol, or other weapon of Harris's choice. Harris declined the offer, but he made a trip to the hardware store, where he purchased the best pistol in stock. His brother W. A. Harris went along, and he too bought a revolver. The brothers began daily practice in gun handling and marksmanship. The cauldron that brews disaster began to boil.

The trouble was not long in coming. On November 19, the judge parked his buggy at Fourth and Austin, which was the chief intersection in downtown Waco. Jim Harris was in front of the drugstore, and his brother Bill was positioned across the street near a boot and shoe store. Both were wearing their guns, but so was the judge.

Jim Harris fired the first shot, but he missed. Judge Gerald got off a shot, and Harris went down. Bill Harris ran across the street firing as he came, and he put two shots into Judge Gerald's back.

A police officer arrived on the scene. Officer Hunt Ballenfant tried to wrestle the pistol from Bill Harris, as Judge Gerald managed to stagger to the site of the struggle between Harris and Ballenfant.

"He shot me in the back!" the judge screamed in outrage as he extended his pistol and put a bullet through Bill Harris's head.

Judge Gerald was taken to the doctor's office, where his mangled arm was amputated and his back wound was ministered to. The judge would later inquire as to where he had shot Jim Harris.

When he was told that his bullet struck Harris's Adam's apple, the judge seemed satisfied.

"I aimed for the s.o.b.'s collar button," he said.

The death of the Harris brothers only heightened the tension around Waco, and Brann's *Iconoclast* did not apply any healing elixir to the situation.

On April 1, 1898, All Fools Day, William Brann was gunned down in the streets of Waco by a Baylor zealot. Tom Davis placed his shot into Brann's back precisely where his suspenders formed an X. Brann, however, was not the only death recorded in that back-shooting incident. He managed to turn, draw his pistol, and take Tom Davis with him.

Tom Davis was a Waco businessman who paid for his back shooting with his life. Both men died within a few hours.

Brann's funeral and burial in Oakwood Cemetery drew a record number of Waco citizens. A few mourners were on hand, but the bulk of the attendance was made up of spectators who simply wished to view the corpse. They wanted to be certain that the hated apostle from hell was actually in the box.

Months passed, and George Crippen, who had lost his gambling hall at the hand of Judge Gerald, was asked whether or not he might now claim vengeance on the judge.

"Brann is dead and in the ground," the questioner pointed out, "and old Judge Gerald ain't got but one good arm. Ain't you tempted to go and even the score?"

"You'll not catch me starting anything with that old man," Crippen responded. "If he lost both arms and both legs he'd bite you to death!"

Judge Gerald died in bed at the age of seventy-nine in 1914, and a headstone was erected above the two spaces allotted to Judge Gerald and his wife. The engraved epitaph states: "It may be oblivion's dreamless sleep, It may be to another and a better life, ¿Quien Sabe? we are content."

Mrs. Gerald occupies her designated space, but the judge engaged a nephew to have his remains cremated and then distribute the ashes in a ten-mile arc of Galveston Bay.

"I just want to see if Saint Peter can gather those bones up when the final trumpet sounds," he told the nephew.

Postscript from Garza

Traveling from the southeast on U.S. 84, you top out on the caprock just before you arrive at Post, Texas, in Garza County. Post had an interesting time back in the early nineteen hundreds—from 1911 through 1914 to be precise. Had Elmer Kelton grown up there during that time, he would have still had inspiration to write his saga of West Texas and *The Time It Didn't Rain.*

Charles William Post, the originator and manufacturer of Post Toasties, got the great notion to grow the main ingredient for his cereal in the sandy soil of Texas, and he was assured by area farmers that you could raise a bumper crop of most anything in Garza County if you added water to the equation.

Charles William sold lots of boxes of cereal and had money in his pocket when he set out to grow corn around Post. He had a theory about rainmaking and the capital to pull it off.

Dynamite blasts, he'd been told, were a sure rain producer. In every war since China patented explosives and put them on the market, troops had been getting soaked when the battle was fiercest and bombs were bursting on air.

Charles William put two and two together and figured that if he circled the Post area with enough detonation positions, he could call his shots and blast rain out of the sky when his corn crop needed a drink.

He designated fifteen such points and set off four pounds of dynamite every four minutes when he needed water and the

165

conditions were right. As the clouds scudded toward the north in the protracted "drys" of July and August, Garza County sounded like a battle zone.

Alas and alack, after three years of blasting and blaspheming, his corn growth seldom reached beer-can height. Charles William had sunk a half-million dollars into the project and yet had not produced rain enough to settle the dust, let alone bring in a crop of Post Toasties.

Besides all that, folks around Post got into the annoying habit of complaining about the noise.

"That snap, crackle, and pop day in and day out keeps my new young'un awake, and it squalls all day long with the colic because of all that blamed racket," reported one housewife.

A representative of rival Kellogg overheard the remark and took a portion of her lament as the name for a new rice cereal.

Holy Ground

It's recorded in the deed records of Polk County, Texas, so the legality and reality of the conveyance is not open for dispute. It is, however, highly unusual.

In 1895 a religious group, remembered only as the New House of Israel, founded a town in Polk County, and once it had acquired the property, its members got busy and erected a place of worship—a practice not unlike the procedure followed by religious factions of most all persuasions who migrated to the fertile acreage of sin-infested Texas back in olden days.

Their activity did not attract much attention until they showed up at the courthouse, paid the fee, and recorded the paperwork necessary to designate ownership. Their entire acreage was deeded to "Lord God of Israel, Creator of Heaven and Earth." No means of contacting the owner in case of a taxing problem was given to the county clerk.

A sheriff's auction in case of taxes falling in arrears would have been an arresting spectacle, but if the situation ever arose, it is not on record.

Old Rip

There was one heap of a tub-thumping all through the month of February to entice the public into bunching up for an event on the courthouse square in the heart of Eastland, Texas. The slogan for the event was "A Sight to Behold!"

The old courthouse was being wrecked in preparation for the edifice you can see today if you don't mind exiting Interstate 20 at Cisco, if you're bound for the Metroplex, or getting off at Eastland if you're westward bound. Old Highway 80 will take you on a scenic cruise through both towns and allow you to stop at the county seat in Eastland and see the proof of what is about to be divulged unto you.

First off, though, you need to know that according to census figures the population of Eastland was 9,368 on February 28, 1928. Fifteen hundred of that number converged upon the site of the courthouse to do a little beholding of the promised spectacle.

Ernest Wood had performed an unusual act to cap off the ceremonies back in 1897, when the original courthouse had been erected. He had placed a young horned frog into a miniature chamber in the cornerstone, and it was then hermetically sealed with mortar, leaving that little reptile without food, water, fresh air, or sunlight. Its only comfort was a King James Bible.

The crowd was there to see that crypt opened after the passage of thirty-one years. Legend opined that horned toads just doze off when they get in a tight place like that and patiently wait for better

169

days. Like the bear that goes into hibernation and waits faithfully
for springtime, and the grit of the TCU Frogs as they endure entire
football seasons without making a first down. Memories of Sam
Baugh and Davey O'Brien are about the only buoys available to
sustain faith in the coming of better seasons. The Fighting Frogs
have been known to doze for years.

Anyways, for the litmus testing of Ernest's prediction, wit-
nesses of impeccable credentials and unquestionable honesty were
also at the ceremony—Reverend F. E. Singleton, County Judge
Edward Prichard, and Mr. Blair Cherry, who was football coach
of the Ranger Bulldogs. He would later be head coach of the UT
Longhorns, so it's obvious that reputable dignitaries were there to
see that no hanky panky was allowed.

Oddly enough, there were two late arrivals that fateful day.
Two flappers passing through Eastland en route from Abilene to
Fort Worth were attracted by the throng of people. Curious, they
stopped their Model T Ford touring car to check out the action.

They could not see over the crowd, but Lizzie climbed onto
the car hood so that she could see what was creating all the ruckus.
Thelma stayed on the ground and allowed Lizzie to report from
her vantage point.

A final section of wall was toppled, and right there in plain
sight was the covering of the horned-frog detention chamber. A
muffled drumroll sounded as Mr. Eugene Day advanced and positioned himself to lift the lid of the masonry coffin.

A hush fell over the crowd as the metal covering was pried
loose, then a hand was thrust into the cavity and retrieved the
Good Book. Slowly and carefully a wriggling little horned toad
was next lifted to freedom. The multitude buzzed with excitement,
and a booming voice rang out the announcement.

"Thirty-one long and darkened years he has slept in the corner
stone!" The voice proclaimed. "He is alive, as you can plainly see,
and ready to renew old acquaintances. Ladies and gentlemen, it is
my pleasure to introduce Old Rip! Make him feel welcome!"

A thunderous wave of applause was instantaneous, and Thel
tugged vigorously at Lizzie's skirt.

"What is it, Lizzie? What's been in that corner stone for thirty-
one years? I couldn't hear what the man said."

"It's a horny toad!" Liz replied in an awe-stricken tone.

"Well, I'm not surprised," Thelma responded. "And," she added, "I'll bet he's hungry, too."

Rip was an instant celebrity, and his fame spread throughout the civilized world. Public appearances were clamored for and made. Rip even made a cameo appearance at the White House in Washington, D.C.

Calvin Coolidge was holding down the presidential post at the time, and Rip was ushered into his presence with great ceremony and was placed upon Calvin's desk for examination and deserved adulation.

Cal stared in silence as the little reptile scurried about, but true to his nickname, spoke nary a word. His out-of-earshot description was justified—Wags referred to him, with little deference, as "Calvin the Silent." Old Rip said as much as President Coolidge.

Time passed, water passed beneath the bridge, and Rip's barnstorming act lasted until he broke a hind leg doing a buck and wing in Hollywood. It was an unfortunate setback for Rip, since he was auditioning for an appearance with Fay Wray.

He lived out his remaining days back home in Eastland

County and is now on display at the courthouse in suitable sur-
roundings. His mummified remains are still an attraction.

Old Rip's post-mortem reputation has diminished with the
passage of time, but a special observance takes place in his hometown on an annual basis.

And as late as June 2002, he was booked as an attraction at
Six Flags Over Texas in Arlington, Texas.

Doing Hard Time

The Roaring Twenties and the good times that had rolled since the end of World War I ceased as abruptly as a mocking bird trying to fly through a plate glass window. On October 24,1929, the stock market suffered total collapse—a day that is remembered even now as Black Thursday, up Wall Street way.

Four-fifths of Texas's population was rural, and the price of stock was of scant importance to them unless you were talking livestock, but within a year's time the money famine had gotten their undivided attention. When the money supply that purchased their farm and ranch produce petered out, many lost their mortgaged lands, tenants lost their jobs, and 70 percent of Texas's workforce fell into the category of the unemployed. When the calendar advanced to the 1930 mark, Texas joined the rest of the nation in welcoming hard times. Over 5 percent of Texas whites were on relief, and about 9 percent of the black population joined them.

Herbert Hoover had been elected president of these United States and had assumed his duties in March of 1929. As time passed without getting any better, he was accorded full blame for the fix the USA was in.

Shantytowns, erected from scraps, that housed the down-and-outs were known as "Hoovervilles"; newspapers were classified as "Hoover Blankets"; and in Texas, jackrabbits and armadillos were tracked down and eaten under the classification of "Hoover Hogs." Freight trains on the rails crisscrossing America moved

chupp '72

more tonnage in hobos than freight. Good working men were riding the rails in search of employment, but most would end up
knocking on back doors and begging for food.

Hoover got the heat for the woeful conditions of the nation,
but Governor Ross Sterling, who had beaten Miriam Ferguson in
a runoff election, also received his fair share of blame.

Hoover and Sterling held a common belief that help for the
nation and the state was possible only by helping business. Sterling,
without asking the legislature, called for a bond issue to improve
the Texas highway system. Such an undertaking would ease the
unemployment for many, he contended.

Sterling arranged for leaders in the cotton-producing states to
convene in Austin and proposed state control of cotton acreage in
an attempt to raise prices and thereby make cotton production a
paying proposition.

Cotton sold for six cents a pound in 1931, and even though
Texas produced over five million bales, the producers lost money.
The Texas legislature enacted the Cotton Acreage Control Law,
which set a limit of 30 percent of any property owner's total acre-

age. The other cotton-producing states agreed to the condition, but they went back home and clean forgot about the meeting. Only Texas was bound, until passage of the Agricultural Adjustment Act of the New Deal. The New Deal did not arrive until Herbert Hoover lost his job to Franklin Delano Roosevelt in 1932.

To make things worse, the Dust Bowl period of the thirties relocated Texas topsoil to different locations, and the migration of rural Texans to cities accelerated.

Discovery of oil in Kilgore was made in 1930 by Columbus "Dad" Joiner, and that strike increased the population of Kilgore to a head count of over five thousand and provided employment in the East Texas piney woods. A thousand wells were drilled within six months, and production climbed to two hundred million barrels by 1933. The production proved to be both a blessing and a curse. Oil prices dropped from a dollar a barrel to a dime.

Governor Sterling's solution was predictable. He asked lease operators to shut down their production, but as could have been expected, his solution was not favorably received by the oil men. Many of the independents vowed to back with guns their right to pump oil. Sterling proclaimed martial law and sent the National Guard, under command of Jacob Walters, to shut down the field.

The fact that Governor Sterling had close ties to Humble Oil and that Jacob Walters had once served as an attorney for that Texas company caused hard feelings and ruffled feathers among those independent oil producers. Suspicions that both Sterling and Walters might possibly be protecting their own interests didn't set well, and discouraging and disparaging words were bandied about.

Subsequently, the East Texas fields were allowed to resume production, but with a "daily allowable" stipulation. That allowable was set at 225 barrels per day per well. Nobody got shot, so the allowable was reduced to a hundred barrels.

Prices crept upward, and so did illegal production. The independents tried manfully to resist the temptation but were unable to stay from running off a little "hot oil" when prices rose and a ready market awaited. Hot oil production, in time, was greater than the legitimate production. Some employees took up the habit too, and they ran off a batch now and again to bootleg and put the proceeds in their individual pockets. Landowners, who theoretically received a royalty on each barrel, were a tad disturbed at those she-nanigans, and they cried out in anguish to the authorities.

The Supreme Court studied over the deal and judged that Governor Sterling had exceeded his constitutional authority in his use of the National Guard. The Railroad Commission's head honcho, a Mr. Ernest Thompson, sent the Texas Rangers to restore order.

Hot oil availability spawned new refineries, and cheaper gasoline was the end result. The East Texas oil producers pumped hot oil, and the price of petroleum products undersold the major producers and caused sleepless nights for Governor Sterling.

In 1932, the voters spurned Sterling's bid for reelection. Ma and Pa Ferguson took the reins once again, and since Texans had had enough of Herbert Hoover too, they joined the national bandwagon and elected Franklin D. Roosevelt as president and CEO of the United States. Texas native son John Nance Garner of Uvalde, who was Speaker of the House, was anointed as vice president. Many Texans felt that the situation up in D.C. would have been more to their liking if Garner was president and Roosevelt was flunky.

Cactus Jack was once asked for his honest opinion of the vice presidential gig, and his response may have shocked many but not the people back home who knew him. "The vice president's job don't amount to much more than a bucket of warm spit," was the doctored quote in the papers, but Garner did not say "warm spit." What he actually said was close—it is a liquid expelled from an orifice of the human anatomy that is situated just below the equator.

Garner pitched in and helped Roosevelt push the New Deal program of relief and recovery through Congress, and the Emergency Banking Act, Agricultural Act, and the National Recovery Act were born. All three were declared unconstitutional by an ultraconservative Supreme Court. Franklin D. was sorely vexed and did his dead-level best to increase the number of justices from nine to fifteen. He theorized that six additional friendly faces of his choice might make it easier to get a little respect. Wishful thinking.

When Roosevelt failed in his attempt to stack the Supreme Court, he managed to father the Civilian Conservation Corps

(CCC), which furnished jobs for young men in conservation projects; the National Youth Administration (NYA), which kept youngsters in school and off the job market; and the Public Works Administration (WPA), which put men to work building schools and bridges (that force was commonly known as the "We Piddle Around" troops, in layman's language). The Old Age Pension began, eventually becoming Social Security. Jesse Jones, of Houston, was a willing doer in these efforts and became Roosevelt's right-hand man. Franklin D. stayed in touch with America via his "fireside chats" on the radio and enjoyed a following of loyal subjects from sea to shining sea. He delivered his inspirational messages without cue cards.

Back in Texas, Governor Sterling grudgingly yielded control to Ma Ferguson. She arrived with "Pa," her almost impeached husband, who had also served as Texas governor until he was apprehended making off with the cookie jar. Ma resumed her lucrative prisoner-pardoning practice for wayward Texans doing time in the state penal colonies.

Other highlights of legislative actions during Ma's term included the legalization of prizefighting and the repeal of the Eighteenth Amendment by ratification of the Twenty-First, repealing statewide prohibition. Texas returned to a system of local option for hard liquor sales. Texans could go to see a boxing match and swill 3.2 beers if they chose and if the particular geographic allowed such goings on.

James Allred won the governorship in 1934 by besting a field of six other aspirants. He combined the Texas Rangers with the Department of Public Safety and won an old-age assistance package for Texans. Allred won a second term in 1936, but when 1938 rolled around he had 20,060 Texans on relief and a hundred thousand working for the Feds. Impatient voters were looking for a change, and they located that change in an unusual personage.

"Pappy" W. Lee O'Daniel came along, riding to the rescue on a hillbilly flour truck. He starred on a noon radio show, which was aired statewide, and in his country way he became as popular as Franklin D. Instead of fireside chats, he presented sacred music with the unashamed participation of his band, which would become the Light Crust Doughboys.

Pappy Lee was selling flour by pushing Poor Richard's Almanac wisdom and down-home music. They toured the state, and Pappy Lee became a household word. He was probably the best-known and recognized man in Texas.

Loyal fans urged him to run for governor, and he shucked and jived his way into the race. His platform was proclaimed as adherence to the Golden Rule and Ten Commandments. His opponents ridiculed his entry, but when the tally was taken W. Lee had 95 percent of the vote and won in a landslide.

Pappy Lee was succeeded by Coke Stevenson, and Coke was reelected twice more and after his retirement from the political arena boasted about his accomplishment of returning Texas to prosperity. But his role may have been as a bit player in the dramatic reversal of fortune.

On December 7, 1941, the Empire of Japan bombed Pearl Harbor, and the world changed.

Texas's Centennial

In 1936, Texas reached its one hundredth year of existence. Republic, Union, Confederacy, and a return to statehood in the United States was the gauntlet Texas had managed to negotiate, and most of the scars from the experience had healed when the initial century elapsed.

The birthday bash was officially headquartered and pulled off in Dallas, Texas, where the Centennial Exposition extended from June 6 through November 29, 1936.

The Official Souvenir Guide extended through 112 pages and featured stirring descriptions of the many exhibits and buildings constructed for the occasion. The Official Souvenir Guide was priced at two bits and was worth every penny.

That World's Fair claimed to show the complete story of "An Empire on Parade," and the price tag came to twenty-five million dollars—a goodly amount of money in 1936.

James V. Allred was Texas's governor of record, and his official welcome to Texas Centennial visitors, reprinted here, is unquestionably worth the price of the official guide:

April 3, 1936
Texas Centennial Year
TO TEXAS CENTENNIAL VISITORS
GREETINGS:

A century ago the Republic of Texas was founded. Born out of war and travail this Southwestern nation achieved a place in the world

179

Official
SOUVENIR
GUIDE

★

25¢

TEXAS CENTENNIAL
EXPOSITION ★ DALLAS
JUNE 6 to NOVEMBER 29

through its recognition by foreign powers. For a decade it existed, a nation on the frontier of the Western World.

Then the people of Texas voluntarily joined the American Union. As the twenty-ninth state of the Union, Texas, with the nation, marched forward. From an outpost of civilized government it has changed into a mighty commonwealth rich in material and social resources, a leader in commerce and industry, a great contributor to all phases of the American scene.

The heritage of liberty and freedom, which belongs to Texas, a gift from the brave men and women of those early days, is truly the heritage of the American people. Here, where the South and West are merged we have another great tradition, that of hospitality. As you visit Texas and the Texas Centennial Exposition to be held in Dallas from June 6 to November 29, be assured that all Texas is your host. We are proud of the State of Texas. We are proud of her great history and great achievements. This year, as Texas celebrates the one-hundredth anniversary of her independence we ask you to share with us in that pride.

Thoroughly Texan, always American, the Texas Centennial Exposition is dedicated to the great past of the Lone Star State. But more than that—it is dedicated to the American people, to every American who, this year joins with Texas in celebrating a great event. To you, on behalf of Texas and her people, I say, "Welcome to AN EMPIRE ON PARADE."

> Cordially yours,
> James V. Allred
> Governor of Texas

The attendees of this celebration were survivors of the Roaring Twenties and, in 1936, prisoners of the Great Money Famine that gripped American by the throat from "sea to shining sea." Texas had fared no better and no worse than the other forty-seven states, but for those who journeyed to Dallas and had the price of admission, the exhibits were indeed wonders to behold and discuss with folks back home in rural Texas who missed the show.

In the Electric Hall, for instance, the innovations of the "Magic Century" were displayed with pride and style. The exhibitors were the Elgin National Watch Company, International Business Machines, Singer Sewing Machine, Western Union, and Westinghouse Electric.

The Elgin display featured details of the Elgin Observatory, with its array of equipment to ensure the accuracy of the Elgin timepiece. Exotic devices such as a three-inch transit telescope, a Reifler precision clock, and a chronograph were all necessary links in the precise time-measuring business. Time signals were emitted by wire and by radio so that watch owners could twist the knob on their watch and recite an exact reading when asked for the right time.

There was a working model of an Elgin watch built to a scale of ten to one. Unwary visitors were often alarmed by the sound of whirring gears and flexing springs of the gargantuan timepiece, since it approximated the sound of an approaching locomotive. It was not uncommon for handheld children to wet their pants at the Elgin exhibit.

Western Union's exhibit thumped the tub for the company's electrically powered telegraph. Its new improved model, perfected in its laboratories, actually told the time of dispatched messages, and the Texas Centennial featured the official debut of that marvelous advance of communication technology. A sneak peek at the newfangled "Electric Eye" was another of the arresting sights, along with stock and news tickers and clocks showing the time in worldwide time zones. Another attraction was an actual "Exposition Telegraph Service," whereby you could send an actual telegram to any part of the country for a small sum. The excitement of a friend or relative receiving a wire saying "I'm at the Texas Centennial Exposition. Wish you were here" is hard to imagine.

The transportation exhibit showcased scale-model reproductions of electric and diesel locomotives, a modern streetcar, and a trolley coach. Little hobos were positioned strategically on these functioning marvels as a reminder that happy days were not epidemic in America.

Westinghouse also displayed the very latest in refrigerators, ranges, dishwashers, water heaters, washing machines, and all manner of lighting devices.

One convenience that may have still been on the drawing board was the clothes dryer. Apparently, the clothesline was still in use in 1936.

International Business Machines had a display of scales,

counting devices, and electric writing machines, along with accounting and bookkeeping devices. The rural folk, who were in the majority attendance-wise, did not spend a lot of time in the study of these wares.

Also in the Electrical Hall was the Eastman Kodak display and the Beacon Book Shop. The book shop's location in that company was hard to figure out back then—and, if you get right down to it, hard to understand today.

Scads of additional attractions were also nestled in the Hall of Communications, the Travel Section, and the Transportation Group.

The crown jewel, however, in the entire spectacular was a panoramic extravaganza. The epic production was best described in the two-bit Official Souvenir Guide and the text follows:

Cavalcade of Texas

The spectacle of an empire marching to its destiny through four hundred years is to be a feature of the Texas Centennial Exposition at Dallas, June 6 to November 29.

This panoramic extravaganza is "Cavalcade of Texas," written and produced as a living saga of the inexorable advance of civilization, blood and iron and the enduring will of the white man in what was once only the wild land of the naked savage.

"Cavalcade of Texas" will be more than a sweeping canvas of a hundred years of Texas independence in this, 1936, the year of its Centennial. It will draw the brush of history, in deep but authentic colors, across the stretch of an empire.

From Pineda, the Spanish explorer of 1519, to President Tyler, who signed the joint resolution of the United States congress admitting Texas into the Union, "Cavalcade of Texas" will, by episodic panorama, recreate Texas history through living characters and realistic scenic effects. It reaches even farther into the present, closing with an episode depicting the first State Fair at Dallas in 1886, with background of silhouettes of skylines of Texas' great modern cities.

Moving across a great stage, 300 by 170 feet, will march the men who shaped the destiny of Texas: Pineda, the first White Man to set foot on the soil of Tejas (Indian for "friendly") of the Indians. Then de Vaca, Coronado, and the other Conquistadores, De Soto,

Espejo, de Onate and those ill-dogged adventurers who sought the mythical golden cities.

La Salle and his doomed ships sail across the stage, De Leon marches in from Mexico. Then, by swift picture and dramatic scenes, the rise and fall of the Mission era is portrayed. Here the opening of the trade route over the San Antonio road is shown.

Next comes Jean Lafitte, of piratic legend, seizing Galveston Island for a base for his buccaneering on the Spanish galleons. And after him the Austins' efforts at colonization.

The thunder of arms is next, the tread of feet of frontiersman hastening across the Sabine to reinforce Texas in her beginning struggle for freedom. The storming of San Antonio, the death of brave Ben Milam, the massacre of the men in the Alamo.

It is all in the "Cavalcade of Texas" with the sharp projection of a film spectacle but with the more graphic intensity of human actors and massive scenes.

The panorama moves forward vividly through changing scenes, larger times, the oncoming of civilization to a virgin land. You see Austin, Houston, Lamar and other immortals of the Lone Star State. The war with Mexico in 1838 and the quieting of boundaries is depicted, and from there the beginning of a new order.

The story is episodic in that it is told in scenes and eras through "cut backs" taken from two central and modern young characters, the inevitable boy and girl. Their wills clash—the girl abominates Texas, the boy, a cowhand, defends it—and the march of an empire springs there before the eyes of the spectators, visitors to the $25,000,000 World's Fair of 1936.

The "Cavalcade of Texas" is much more than a pageant. It is a mighty spoken drama of perhaps the most glamorous and romantic epochs in the history of the winning of the West—a West never to be seen again save through the play and the players, "Cavalcade of Texas."

"Special admission days" were observed on each Tuesday. The customers of kid caliber were admitted for a single buffalo nickel.

Most tourists and aliens to Big D sighted in on Magnolia's winged Red Horse. Pegasus rotated slowly atop the tallest building in Dallas.

The blowout was worth seeing, but of course there's an upside if you missed out due to not yet being born. You have longer to live now than if you'd attended.

Tiger

The Johnson Space Center just happened to wind up down around Houston. The fact that old Lyndon was running the nation did not enter into the area designation, or for that matter, inspire the name.

The plain fact of the matter is, Texas has more airspace than any other of the fifty states to operate in. While it's true that Alaska has more acreage, a lot of it is unusable for aviating because of all that snow and ice, and all those mountains sticking up all over the place. Texas does not have those drawbacks, and that's why it has merited its monopoly of things aerial.

Claire Lee Chennault was not born in Paris, as you might suspect from the family name. Instead, Claire was born and grew up fifty or so miles south of Paris, back in 1890. Another conclusion you might possibly come to would also be in error. Claire was born in Commerce, over in the piney woods of East Texas, and Paris is, naturally, also situated in Texas. And Claire Lee Chennault was not of the feminine persuasion.

Recognizing how much sky it took to cover his home state, Claire opted to take up the trade of aviator. He served in World War I with the U.S. Army Air Service and found that frequent flying was a thing he enjoyed. He kept plying his avocation and at the age of forty signed on with Chiang Kai-shek, who was a Chinese general in charge of the Chinese air force. Hitler et al. were creating an uproar over in Europe, and Japan was beginning to rattle swords. World War II was nearing, and General Chiang was fortunate in his hiring of Major General Chennault to aid and abet him in the organization and training of an air force to protect Chinese skies.

Chennault assembled a volunteer group of better than 250 men, as a training team for the Chinese cadets, who would become expert combat pilots and win world acclaim for their exploits in battle. They called the outfit "Flying Tigers," and they inspired many a movie with their derring-do and their P-40 planes with the sharp painted teeth on either side of their single-engine fuselages.

They were charged with the mission of holding back the Japanese invasion of China. Which they did.

The fabled force metamorphosed into the Fourteenth Air Force in 1943, after America's forced entry into the fray.

Weathering the Worst

If I owned Hell and Texas I'd live in Hell and rent out Texas," an early appraisal of our Lone Star State, is famous the length and breadth of our forty-seven other contiguous states and our two disassociated members of the United States. It is branded as infamous raving by bona fide residents, of course, even though there are times when some would tend to agree.

The most recent conversion to that rating occurred back in 1980, when summer began with three-digit temperatures and maintained such readings in a streak that endured until autumn arrived. The electric utility companies did not complain, but the consumers squealed like pigs caught under a gate. Until that record is topped, the survivors will brag about how they outlasted the warm spell, and the severity of the ordeal will be taught in Texas history. It has not yet been long enough to be a topic of ancient history, but it's getting there.

That torrid trial of endurance is not unique in trying men's and women's souls by any means, though. It honestly may not even make the top ten. For instance, the very first printed report of weather was distributed to the Texas population on, July 15, 1859. To wit:

> Oppressive Heat—The weather was cloudy last night, and bright flashes of lightning, accompanied by the distant roar of thunder showed there was a storm brewing somewhere. We looked at every

moment for a tremendous shower, but the night passed without a drop of rain. The atmosphere was quiet, oppressive—enough so to make one very restless.

This morning the sun is bright and hot; and the whitish, heavy clouds, that hang low on the horizon, moving slowly and growing darker as they move, seem to increase the heat instead of tempering it. We are bound to have rain, but how soon? Is the question Mean while we suffer intolerable heat and are kept in a state of continual perspiration. A light breeze now and then finds its way from among the clouds, and sends us a refreshing puff, which barely keeps us alive.

Sounds like the inspiration for Elmer Kelton's early publication, doesn't it? Not so, Elmer drew his story line from the Crane County territory where he grew up.

When Cabeza de Vaca made his first appearance in Texas, he was regarded as a deity of some magnitude by the sod-busting Indians, who nested down near the present city of Persidio. They'd been rain dancing for two years at the time, and all they'd gotten for their efforts were sore feet.

The least amount of rain to fall, on a statewide average, was a piddling 14.30 inches back in 1917, but that figure was of flood dimensions to many areas that held the figure in check, despite Houston's usual flood-producing allotment.

In contrast, 1941's rainfall was a whopping 42.62 average; in 1921, Thrall in Williamson County fell heir to 36.40 inches in an eighteen-hour downpour; and back in 1893, Clarksville had an annual rainfall of 109.38 inches.

Medicine shows waned in popularity during the tail end of the 1800s, and a new and exotic breed of con men hustled the thirsty sections of Texas, accepting fees and promising rain. Rainmakers came with their hands extended—palms up, of course.

Civil War veterans were of the opinion that heavy artillery bombardments triggered the celestial rainmaking apparatus, and in 1891 a cannon was positioned on the parched acres of the King Ranch down in South Texas. Balloons were released with magical elixirs encased, and when they achieved the most advantageous altitude, they were summarily blasted with a cannon ball. Of course it worked, but it took its own good time getting it done, and the rainmaker took all the credit.

A monumental dry spell set in back in the 1950s, moving from west to east, and it spanned the decade. Only ten of Texas's 254 counties were spared; all the rest were declared disaster areas.

Now, if you've got the notion that Texas never gets enough rain, the spring and early summer of 2002 should dispel that myth. On a single day, San Antonio received more than a foot and a half of rainfall. Most areas east of Abilene had their annual rations within a few days. From Abilene to El Paso it was an entirely different story. The wind blew, and the sand flew. In 1956, Wink, Texas, established the dubious all-time record for low tide by getting only 1.76 inches.

Springtime in Texas sometimes produces hailstones of remarkable dimension. On May 8, 1926, outlying areas of Dallas saw hail that measured a foot in circumference. Not to be outdone, San Antonio had the ground covered with grapefruit-dimension orbs of ice, and in 1973, the East Texas city of Conroe had a peppering of hail that measured two feet.

Once in a while the barbed-wire fence that keeps Alaskan snow at bay breaks a strand, and the resulting breach of security can cause unnerving developments all the way from Amarillo to Galveston. In February of 1899, the temperature dropped to minus twenty-three degrees at Tulia, and a dash to Padre Island would have afforded scant relief. Galveston registered a tad more than seven degrees, and the bay had a skim of ice.

Maybe that cynical hater of Texas had a point when he chose hell as his home place and opted to rent out Texas.

Unbroken Circle

Lucky Lady II lifted off the runway at Carswell Air Force base at 11:21 A.M. on Wednesday, February 26, 1949. The *Lucky Lady* was a B-50 Superfortress, piloted by Captain James Gallagher with a crew of fourteen.

The mission was a circumnavigation of the globe, following the equator. The distance figured out at 23,452 miles, and the trip was made without touching down for fuel. This magic was accomplished by four midair transfusions from flying tanker B-29s. Lieutenant General Curtis LeMay was very secretive concerning the refueling maneuver. "It's something the United States will keep to itself as long as possible," he stated.

The *Lucky Lady* was refilled over Lagens, in the Azores; Dhahran, Saudi Arabia; Clark Air Force Base, Manila; and Hickam Air Force Base in Hawaii.

On March 2, the *Lucky Lady* was back on the ground at Carswell Air Force Base in Fort Worth, Texas. It had averaged a speed of 249 mph and clocked in from its circuit of the planet in ninety-four hours and one minute. The estimated arrival time had been calculated for 9:24, but the *Lucky Lady* beat the estimate by two full minutes. Captain Gallagher was all smiles when he heard about the two minutes he and his crew had shaved off the educated estimate.

"It was a team effort which produced this amazing statistic," he said. "We just flew our plane one mile at a time to achieve this outstanding result." General LeMay, Strategic Air Command *hefe grande,* beamed with pride and shared in the spotlight and the glory.

His fame had already been well established when he directed the firebombing and the deposit of atomic bombs on Hiroshima and Nagasaki back in the forties. That event took most of the starch out of Japan's ambition to get control of more real estate. General LeMay was humble but pleased at the ensuing result—the surrender of the Empire of Japan.

"This means that we can now deliver an atomic bomb to any place in the world that requires an atomic bomb!" General LeMay chortled proudly.

There were no reported requisitions.

Happy Got Lucky

Snowbirds of varying plumage flock along the east bank of the Rio Grande on an annual basis. Bird spotters along that stretch of wild country from El Paso to the Gulf welcome the influx of winter nesters with open arms and hands extended in friendship—palm up, of course—and doing as the Good Book advises. If they see a stranger, they take him in.

Del Rio is one of the favorite nesting places for whiling away the winter months for the northern migratory species, and a trip across the bridge will put the adventuresome visitors in the land of the amigo, where the reception is much the same but worded a tad differently. Their slogan: "You can fleece a sheep twice a year, but you can only skin him once!" Cuidad Acuna has attractions to satisfy any yen.

Kinney County adjoins Val Verde and features an attraction most visitors include in their "must see" agenda. Smack dab in the middle of Kinney County is Bracketville, thirty-two miles southeast of Del Rio, and it has the distinction of being one of the most utilized movie sets in Texas.

Happy Shahan was the man with the plan and the grit to get off his haunches when Fort Clark was shut down by the U.S. Army in 1944. He hustled Hollywood. When the army went rolling away, Bracketville lost half its population and better than 90 percent of its cash flow. Happy, true to his name, kept his enthusiasm during the dark hours when the town seemed doomed to extinction. In 1950,

Happy was mayor and set about convincing the city council that Hollywood filmmakers were always on the prod for locales to shoot the then-popular westerns. They scoffed at Happy's proposal, but he was not deterred and forthwith lit a shuck for Hollywood.

"I'll be back in ten days," he told his wife, Virginia. "I don't know anything about making movies, but I know how to talk to people who do."

On the final day, Happy gained admittance to the Disney Studios and came back to Bracketville with a commitment for the movie *Arrowhead*. It featured Jack Palance, Brian Keith, and Charlton Heston, and it put Bracketville on the map for many a western saga.

The biggie, of course, was John Wayne's *Alamo*, and during construction of that structure, Alamo Village was also done.

Of course they blew up the Alamo for the landmark movie, but the town survived, and Alamo Village drew paying guests from all over the planet. The snowbird attendance alone amounted to a formidable number, and movie production became a year-round business.

To accommodate the tourist trade, Happy presented a musical program and a shoot-out on Main Street several times a day. Alamo Village drew more of a crowd than Bracketville.

An elderly couple from Pennsylvania trekked to the ruins of the Alamo and stared in awe and reverence for the longest time. Their hands joined, and the man looked at his wife of many years.

"That is all that remains of the shrine of Texas independence. Many brave men made the ultimate sacrifice within those shattered walls," he said. She listened intently, tears welled in her eyes, and she blotted them away with a tissue.

"What do you think of our Alamo Village?" Happy Shahan walked up and joined the couple.

"I guess that it's only fitting that this cradle of Texas liberty be left in shambles," the elderly Penn Stater said. "Much of the drama would be lost if repairs and restoration were done, I expect."

"You're probably right," Happy agreed. "It would certainly be an undertaking to try and raise that Phoenix from the ashes. I plan to leave it as it is!"

"I would have loved to see it back before the battle," the wife again daubed at her eyes.

"I can see that you folks are tourists from out of state, and I don't mean to pry, but do you have plans to go to San Antonio and take in the sights down that way?" Happy asked.

"Yes, as a matter of fact, that is where we are going when we leave here."

"Well," Happy said, "when you get there, ask around for directions and go and see the Alamo they've got set up there for tourists. It's an exact replica, and they have guided tours."

Bats and Balloons

Desdemona, aka Hogtown, ain't much more than a blister where Highways 8 and 16 intersect in the post-oak thickets nigh the southeastern corner of Eastland County. The blinking light at that intersection pretty much constitutes the night life visible to tourists, who have probably lost their way. The same appraisal sums up the daily action too, to be brutally frank about it. The census claims there are 180 or so inhabitants, and so far nobody has disputed the count.

Ah, but once upon a time things were a lot different on the south bank of Hog Creek. On September 2, 1918, at a depth of 3,500 feet, the Duke Well belched forth a flow of gas, which immediately ignited, and the resulting flames were visible thirty miles away. When the gas pressure petered out, oil followed at a volume of six thousand barrels a day.

Speculators, lease men, and other assorted shysters swooped down on Desdemona like a bald eagle on a trout. Fence posts all over the county were pulled up, and the holes were deepened to oil depth. By January of 1919, the Desdemona field was producing nine hundred thousand barrels of crude per day, and the good times rolled.

Clark Gable and Spencer Tracy starred in a spectacular block-busting movie titled *Boom Town,* and film crews converged on the wilds of central Texas to accumulate background scenes and other supporting footage for the real, true-life look of a boomtown.

Clark and Spencer both said they'd like to see the carnage in person, but conflicting appointments kept 'em in Hollywood.

Welsir, the high old times ran out in 1925, and the movers and shakers shook hands with one another and moved on. Most of the locals were reduced to "working for peanuts" status, which is still practiced unto this day. The oil boom and the film crews were soon forgotten, and when the working girls began their mass migration, Desdemonites went back to drinking creek water and sopping ten-weight gravy.

Time passed, water went under the bridge, and the birds sang. Halcyon days and nights enveloped the area with the density of a London fog, but there was yet another date with destiny for Hog Town, and it occurred on March 23, 1945.

The ranks of those who can remember December 7, 1941, and those of you who saw *Tora! Tora! Tora!* know that the American outpost in Hawaii was set upon, in a sneak attack, by the then Evil Empire of Japan. America responded by entering World War II, and just for good measure we added Italy and Germany to the hit list. We threw in with the Allies, and you all know how it wound up.

By 1944 the war was in its final stages and the Axis was tottering on its last legs, but the Japanese were not inclined to throw in the towel and admit they'd been bested.

Emperor Hirohito's birth date is on November 4, and he was presented an amazing gift on that date in 1944. Instead of candles to blow out, he and the well-wishers who congregated on the east coast of Japan were presented with three hundred balloons, and we're not talking Wally World merchandise here. These were full size, with the dangling gondolas to accommodate payloads, and they were decorated with the rising-sun logo in full color on top. They were fashioned from five plies of paraffin-coated rice paper and inflated with hydrogen.

At the launch site, they were loaded with four incendiaries and a thirty-three-pound fragmentary antipersonnel bomb. Then, much to Hirohito's delight, they were released, rose thirty thousand feet, and entered the jet stream. Immediately, they made a bee-line, at speeds ranging from eighty to 120 miles per hour, for targets in America. They streaked across water and land, and one of them had Desdemona's name on it.

At a site in Oregon, a plaque was later erected to commemorate their effectiveness. "The only place on the American continent where death resulted from enemy action during World War II," that plaque states. A minister, his wife, and a group of children, enjoying a picnic, were the victims.

Pug Guthry was a lad of fifteen years and enrolled in the Desdemona educational facility on March 23, 1945. A glance out the school bus window revealed an uncommon sight to his boyish eyes, and it was evident that the strange contraption was losing altitude. When he gained exit at his rural home, he threw his books on the porch and struck out on a dead run to inspect the unidentified visitor from the blue. He was one of the early arrivals, but he was not the only one at the scene. That balloon drew a goodly crowd.

The balloon deflated on contact, and the paper cover was shredded by the landing.

"There was a strong smell—I think it may have been creosote," Pug, who still lives near Desdemona, will tell you.

The more adventuresome boys in the crowd toted away sections of the balloon and the grass harness ropes. Luckily for the collectors, all bombs had already been dispensed. Three blasts had been reported in and around De Leon, Dublin, and Brownwood, but the military took measures to prevent any widespread dissemination of the news.

Government officials made an early morning call next day at the schoolhouse and gathered all the evidence that had been toted away from the scene. Official word of the incident was not released until war's end. Turns out, balloons were sighted from California to Detroit, Michigan, but our air force could not bring them down. One pilot reported that he climbed to seventeen thousand feet and was still well below the balloon, whose speed he could not match.

It's possible some of those bombs were meant to lay waste to Ney Cave, over close to Bergheim in Kendall County, Texas. That cave was under armed guard and was a training ground for an American armada of ballistic bats.

The Mexican free-tail bats that hung out there were in around-the-clock training, as a strike force against the Empire of

Japan. Government scientists could net those bats, chill them to dormancy, and affix miniature incendiary bombs to their bodies. Then they could be dropped in clusters of five thousand over Japanese cities, and as the warm air revived them they'd fan out and usher in a hot time for the old towns. Tests in the desert had proven successful, so we knew it would work. The Banzai Balloon assault team put that operation in high gear, and the bats were being outfitted with their exploding mechanisms when a strange thing saved their little necks.

On August 6, 1945, *Enola Gay* dropped the first atomic bomb on Hiroshima, Japan, and another followed on August 9 in Nagasaki.

The Mexican free-tail bats received honorable discharges, and presumably all their lighters were reclaimed.

Sometimes when we have a rash of fires around Texas with no reasonable explanation though, it kind of makes one wonder if we taught those bats a bad habit.

Torero-ette

Bull shooting" is an art form that recognizes no boundaries. It is practiced in every climate, every language, and may be a continuous thread in the tapestry of human history.

Oddly, the term is applied exclusively to male gatherings. Of course, women get together and lie, exaggerate, and spin yarns just like men, but "bull shooting" is seldom affixed to or admitted by females. Their verbal exchanges are chats, teas, or gossip fests. These terms are a little gentler than "bull shooting," but the ingredients are the same. And the manly art of bull fighting was also restricted to males for a long, long time.

That's only the tip of the iceberg when you consider the double standards that put the man down and elevate the woman to a lofty perch. Yet another glaring example is practiced by the petroleum industries of our nation. Their restrooms are tagged "Men" and "Ladies" in far too many gas stations. The myth perpetuated here is that most females are ladies, and there are dang few gentlemen amongst the men.

Which is probably true.

Toreador comes from the Spanish *torear* and literally means "to fight bulls."

Torero is the name applied to any member of the *cuadrilla*. The *cuadrilla* includes the matador and assistant assassins, who actually enter the ring to do battle with Toro.

The matador is the one afoot with the cape and the sharp

chuppoz

objects. *Matador* comes from the Spanish *matra,* which is translated simply "to kill." This spectacle, along with pitting dogs and poultry, is illegal in Texas, and none of the three are Olympic events.

Expertise, especially in the gentle art of bull fighting, is a hard commodity to come by north of the border. The sport is appreciated, practiced, and condoned chiefly in Spanish speaking countries and is practiced chiefly by men with a fetish for bull ears.

On January 20, 1952, at the bull ring in Juarez, Mexico, the stands were packed and tortillas sales were brisk. The fans were in a festive mood, but a hush fell upon that assembly when a lady toreador was announced.

She entered the ring and, to the consternation of all, slew two brave bulls.

Patricia McCormack of Big Spring, Texas, was the first lady bullfighter produced by these United States.

Outlying Settlements

Granbury lies near the center of Hood County, while Hico lies in the northeast corner of Hamilton County, but their geographical lying pales when you consider the other lying they indulge in. At least that's the contention of historians and academics of pedigree.

Granbury, you see, claims that John Wilkes Booth and Jesse James occupy separate plots in their graveyard. Cast-iron proofs of those remarkable assertions are not regarded as trivial or concocted by knowledgeable residents and citizens of that expanding city of better than five thousand souls. Many of the businesses around the square have old newspapers and other documents to convince anybody with a thirst for knowledge and a blind trust in printed matter.

When John Wilkes did his dastardly deed in Ford's Theater up in Washington, D. of C., on President Abe Lincoln, he didn't let any grass grow beneath his feet. He got the heck out of town with all due alacrity.

Hysteria reigned throughout the land, and some poor soul was snuffed by law-abiding folk of the time and was planted with faulty information on his grave up in Yankee territory. At least, that's the contention of the congregation down Granbury way.

The second secret burial at Granbury was that of Jesse James, and despite the carping up Missouri way, there's indications that the "Show Me" State ran the risk of being showed, and the incident occurred after the dawn of our brand-new century.

A fact-finding coalition of searchers prevailed to seek the truth of those rumors, and Jesse's remains were exhumed for the performance of DNA testing. The entire nation nervously awaited the results of the scientific determination, and the wait was lengthy enough to be accorded bountiful tub-thumping by the major television networks.

The tests were finally performed, and the results arrived in Granbury—they were negative. The city of Granbury was sorely disappointed and vexed a good deal. The grave was reoccupied with the remains of that unknown person, but the matter was not settled.

Doubters came forth with undisputable evidence that due to a faulty plot map the wrong grave had been exhumed. A motion to try another location in the cemetery was tabled for additional study, so, like Yogi used to say, "It ain't over until it's over."

One disappointed Granburite faulted the establishment for not checking further into the testing.

"They might of dug up John Wilkes Booth for all we know," he opined. "They should a run them tests while they had the chance. At least, we would not have to dig that box up again."

And Granbury stands by its guns—the claim for the last remains of John and Jesse is as strong today as it was fifty years ago. Bear in mind, they have tangible evidence to support both claims. True, the newspapers were published in Granbury, but inked paper is about as dependable as DNA testing and totes more weight with ordinary folk.

Hico was home to William Bonney long after Pat Garret said that he'd filled Billy the Kid with lead out in the wilds of New Mexico.

Brushy Bill was around Hico for many years, and once the statue of limitations went into effect, he quit denying his real and true identity as Billy the Kid. As evidence he could show the scars that he accumulated in his life as the bad boy of Lincoln County. He was as quick as Lyndon Johnson, who would show off his gall bladder procedure scar. And many people aver that very little of his gall was removed.

A museum flourishes in downtown Hico, and they've got

more convincing evidence for tourists to marvel at than can be carted away in a flatbed wagon.

Brushy Bill has passed on, and the pardon he desperately solicited from New Mexico's governor must have got lost in the mail. *¿Quien Sabe?*

Granbury and Hico, although not openly hostile, one with the other, may be the outlyingest towns in the Lone Star State.

Granbury had an ace in the hole once upon a time, but they may have fiddled around too long to show it. Elizabeth Patton Crockett, wife of Davy Crockett, is interred at Acton State Park just outside Granbury, but Granbury may have lost any valid claim to being her eternal resting place. Acton is growing like a cockle burr, and that city-to-be encompasses the smallest state park in existence. It measures twelve by twenty-one feet and contains .006 acre, or as legal document preparers like to say, more or less.

Hico is not out of the game by any means either. Rumors that Elvis is now a tax-paying citizen of that fair city crop up from time to time. Of course, the name he's now operating under is of the hush-hush variety, but you can bet your boots Hico has not folded its cards and left the table.

High Falutin' Evolutin'

They were good old Texas boys who were drafted to go where no man had gone before, and they made their maiden voyage in May of 1959. They first saw daylight in Texas and were raised and trained specifically for the arduous mission and became the pioneers in a technology that became the fetish of the civilized world.

Abel and Baker were the first astronauts. Many people who gathered for blastoff assumed they hailed from Texas A & M, judging by the look of 'em, but those folks were dead wrong. Looks can be deceiving, and Abel and Baker proved the truth of that adage when they flashed the "hook 'em, Horns" hand gesture as they boarded their spacecraft and rocketed into history. They were not the first spaced-out Texans, but they were the first Texans out in space.

On December 4th of that same year, a fraternity brother, Sam, made a solo flight and test piloted the Mercury capsule, which would later carry astronauts into deep space.

Sam put the Mercury through its paces, and it was pronounced spaceworthy when he splash-landed safely in the Atlantic. He returned to Austin and received a hero's welcome and a ticker-tape parade. Governor Price Daniel accompanied Sam in a Mercury convertible and upon arrival at the capitol presented Sam with a magnificent stalk of hothouse bananas.

Abel, Baker, and Sam, in case you're wondering, were Rhesus monkeys and grew up in the Balcones Research Center at the University of Texas.

Now you know why some observers mistook them for Aggies. And, of course, it should be noted that Darwin's theory of evolution was made a little more reasonable and palatable by the derring-do of those simian conquerors of space. For the second time, they blazed the trail that mankind would follow—at least, according to Darwin.

Tale of Two Cities

A demise by "friendly fire" is just as permanent as one that is induced by "enemy fire," but the differentiation is commonly used in reporting battlefield casualties of rival nations.

America is a great hand at volunteering to referee and quite often participate in such disagreements around the globe. Our batting average in that sport falls well below that established by Ted Williams, but we never find a quitting place.

Once upon a time, back near the middle of the 1960s, semi-friendly dialog between the upstart cities of the Permian Basin ensued when state sanction for a branch office was granted for the area. The friendly aspect of the discussion hit low ebb when a precise location for that institution rose to the top of the agenda.

It was mostly through the efforts of Odessa and its citizenry that the longtime dream of a senior college for the Permian Basin was funded and ready to hit the road to reality. Once the money was appropriated, site selection drew the full attention of Odessans and suddenly the interest of Midlanders. During the long crusade, Odessa had manned the front line, but with success assured, Midland arose willing and ready to aid in the placement of the University of Texas in the Permian Basin. Midland contended that the college should be situated near the midway point between Midland and Odessa—a logical conclusion to be sure, unless you happen to own a map.

Odessa's center is around five miles from the east line of Ector

County, thereby putting about fifteen miles between that line and downtown Midland. Since those population centers are separated by only twenty miles and a survey line, it does not require a degree in mathematics to cipher out which county would wind up as beneficiary by a halfway-mark position.

The Odessans rose up in righteous indignation, and they did not bear their displeasure in silence. The Midlanders did their dead-level best to reason with them, but Reason is a poor gladiator to place in the arena with Emotion.

Town hall meetings were rampant in the area. Magnificent Midland and Outrageous Odessa bared their fangs and glared at each other across the twenty-mile stretch of mesquite bushes, which kept them separate and apart. That division was as acute as the one that created the Rebels and the Yankees.

At one semi-organized get-together held at Floyd Gwen Auditorium in Odessa, the crowd overflowed the seating facilities, the standing room, and half-filled the city park outside. Both sides had gifted orators on hand to laud a location for the senior college yet to be constructed.

The speakers alternated between the "Fers" and the "Agins," and the crowd reacted according to the private dictates of their heart.

One exceedingly loud-mouthed Odessan countered Midland entreaties with derision in a tone and volume that was audible throughout the vast Permian Basin. Not only was he in favor of an Ector County site but he wanted the location to be Notrees, which was to the west and halfway to Kermit.

Midland's ace spokesman took the rostrum. He had all the earmarks of a genuine scholar, clad in a wash-and-wear suit, white shirt and tie, and horn-rim glasses. His speech was typed, his papers were in proper order, and his dulcet tone was almost mesmerizing. Even Odessa's leather-lunged critic fell silent.

"It is not ethically or morally right to require Midland students to travel twenty miles to attend the University of Texas in the Permian Basin. Such an arrangement would also be poor business. A location 'between' our two cities is mandatory if this educational facility is to succeed." He paused for a sip of water and allowed the congregation ample time to absorb that data.

"I personally harbor serious doubts concerning Odessa's ability to support a four-year college by itself!" He gathered his papers and smiled at the assemblage; a spasmodic response of sparse applause ensued.

At that point, Odessa's champion of resistance rose to his full height on the back row. He held up both hands for silence and smiled broadly at the gathering. The Midland speaker stopped in midstride and awaited what he prayed was a question.

"There's enough ignorance in Odessa to support an eight-year college!" he bellowed. His name was Warren Burnette, a famous and infamous lawyer in Odessa.

The University of Texas of the Permian Basin is located in Ector County.

Interred in Style

The terms of her handwritten will were observed to the letter.

Sandra Ilene West was buried at San Antonio, Texas, on May 18, 1977, and her casket was a blue 1964 Ferrari. She reportedly wore a silver lace nightgown and sat in the slanted backseat of her beloved automobile. The car was enclosed in a long wooden box, which was lowered into the grave and covered with concrete.

The burial, to be sure, was unusual and worthy of note, but something of equal astonishment awaits an archeologist of the distant future. The passing of the centuries tends to alter cemeteries, and they eventually become excavation sites, "digs." Tombs of the pharaohs and burying grounds of other ancient cultures have provided our modern-day scholars with most of our knowledge and understanding of those "who went before." We who are awaiting our turn now can expect no different treatment in the eons to come.

It would be interesting to witness the disinterment of that blue Ferrari. The license plate and inspection sticker will probably aid in the carbon dating of that exciting find, and scholarly papers will surely emanate from the discoverer.

The sheath of concrete may preserve the automobile as well as it did Old Rip, and if the battery is a Never Fail, the engine might even crank.

Those same archeologists will no doubt puzzle over yet another bizarre trend of burials unearthed in cemeteries of the twentieth century. They will most likely be stupefied and hard pressed to offer a logical explanation for a remarkable constant accompanying male burials. The strip of brightly colored cloth knotted around most throats will surely trigger head scratching and speculation.

Strange explanations are going to be offered as to why so many of the men were choked to death.

Puttin' Al Down

There were over a hundred mourners in attendance on April 28, 1978, when they put Big Al in the ground. Much like Big John, eulogized so poetically by Jimmy Dean, Big Al was an imposing figure, and nobody gave him any lip, either.

Big John, you may remember, cast his lot with coal miners, but Big Al spent his time near Lone Star Steel in Lone Star, Texas. The fainthearted do not labor in either of those trades.

"I didn't even know he was sick."

"Never heard him complain."

"He was the same every day."

"He could eat a horse."

"Rougher than a cob!"

"Could swim like a fish."

"I'm gonna miss ol' Al!"

These were some of the remarks made as Big Al was laid to rest near the Chapel of the Pines. Tears were in evidence on more than one tanned, grizzled cheek as the services proceeded.

Despite the magnitude of that gathering, not a single relative to Big Al was in attendance. No one knew how to get in touch with Big Al's blood kin. It's a sad commentary on our times—we may have daily contact with another being and yet know precious little of his personal life.

The minister spoke reverently of the respect and esteem Big Al had earned from those gathered—steel-making men. No one could recall or remember any variance in Big Al's disposition.

The honor guard stood stiffly erect, sad music came in a flood, and Big Al's handmade pine coffin was slowly lowered into the grave. A melancholy bugle sounded Taps.

A simple pine marker was situated at the head of the grave with hand engraving. It read: "Big Al—April 28, 1978."

Sometimes an accurate description can be found in a name: Little Jimmy Dickens is unbig, Too Tall Jones is tall too, and Dolly Parton definitely is!

Welsir, Big Al was aptly named, too. His casket measured fourteen feet in length, and his five-foot-deep grave was sixteen feet long. Hereafter, when tall Texans are spoken of, Big Al should be in the top ten.

Following the ceremony, the mourners repaired to the shade of the surrounding pines and in hushed tones toasted Big Al for the last time. Sadly they raised their brimming glasses of Gatorade and drained them to the last drop.

Big Al, if you have not already guessed, was a twelve-foot alligator who made his home in the water surrounding the steel plant.

Town Renown

Ysleta was swallowed up by an expanding El Paso, but it is probably the granddaddy of settled population centers in Texas. It was originated in 1682, and the settlers were on the lam due to Indian troubles up north in the present state of New Mexico. Ysleta was and is located on the east bank of the Rio Grande and was home to both Spanish and Indian people who wanted a little peace and quiet. But since they didn't incorporate or do any rezoning, Ysleta is not known as the earliest "town."

Anaqua, whose name fittingly begins with the letter A, was the first settlement to have an assigned name, rank, and serial number. Cabeza de Vaca did the honors, and the name and town stuck in place. When Anglo-Saxons came there in 1836 they most likely had difficulty in pronouncing the name of their hometown, but they didn't see any reason to change it. "It looks as much like an Anaqua as any place in the state," they reasoned, but at a later date it became Anahuac.

Sabine City is lowest in elevation of all Texas cities and towns. Main Street is around eight feet above sea level, and the town folks are wary of any rise in the Gulf whether the rise is due to stormy weather or the thaw of icebergs up in Alaska. There are people around Sabine City who are taller than the town's height above sea level.

If you picture Texas as an irregularly shaped print, you'll realize that a matted and framed specimen, observing the precise configuration, would be a piece of work.

Brownsville, in Cameron County, is as far south as a person can go without getting shark bit and wet.

Away up north is the location of Perryton, and it is the seat of government in Ochiltree County. The land area figures out at around 917 square miles. If the population were evenly distributed, there'd be approximately ten folk to the square mile. With the behavior of upper Texas wind being what it is, they do not have a problem with smog.

Orange is on the easternmost border and is located just east of the Sabine River. It was founded in 1836 when Texas became a republic but was originally named Green's Bluff. The name change took place in 1858.

El Paso had to relinquish its claim as the western edge of Texas in 1952. Anthony expanded the state westward with its incorporation and most likely will always hold the distinction.

Texarkana will complicate the framing job for a Texas print. It, of course, siphoned off its first three letters from Texas, took the "ark" from Arkansas, and finished off with the "ana" tail end of Louisiana. It's the only city named for three parent states.

Thurber, at the northwest corner of Erath County, held an unusual distinction before coal faded as the preferred power source for railroad locomotives and worker strikes made the coal-mining bottom line chancy. The mines were opened in 1886 and were operated by Texas Pacific Oil. Edgar Morston was president of the company in 1903, when a decisive work stoppage ensued from a called strike.

In desperation, the worker's demands were met, and Thurber became the first and possibly only 100 percent unionized town in the world. The railroads switched to alternate fuels, and today the mines lie dormant and wait for future developments.

Spasmodic confrontations between the forces of wets and drys have been common in Texas.

There are those who are convinced that strong drink is the nectar of the devil and the ruination of the human race. Those who fancy a little snort now and again stand firm in their conviction that though strong drink might be man's worst enemy, the Bible urges us to love our enemies.

The sparse population inhabiting the town of Davilla in Milam County has the imposed neutrality of Switzerland. That fact is due to the action of one H. C. Chamberlain, who owned the real estate of Davilla town site, laid out the town plan, and sold lots with the restriction that no intoxicants could ever be sold there.

Fort Worth is the recognized champion when you get right down to the name-calling. In sequential order it has been known as Fort Worth, Fort Town, Stagecoach Town, Cowtown, Panther City, City of Beautiful Heights, Queen City of the Prairies, Where the West Begins (and the pavement ends), Amon Carterville, Arsenal of Democracy, and the City of Lakes.

Although the Chamber of Commerce fails to include the information, Fort Worth was known as Hell's Half-Acre by thirsty and love-starved cattle drovers back in the days when the beef shipment railhead at Cowtown was the market place for cattle.

Milford, Texas, operates under the claim of being "The Home of 700 Friendly People and Three or Four Old Grouches."

Stanton, situated in Martin County in West Texas, makes a similar claim, "Home of 3,000 Friendly People and a Few Old Soreheads." You'd be surprised at the four-letter word that is substituted for "sore" on Stanton's billboard sometimes in the dark of the moon.

When creation was might near completed, God commanded, "Let there be light." The word finally got out to Dell City, just west of El Capitan in Hudspeth County, in 1954, when Rio Grande Electric Co-op ran electric lines to the last city in Texas to get electric service.

Most residents were overjoyed, but old Fred Basset was forced to file for Chapter 11 relief. He'd peddled kerosene for the lamps but had not saved back any of the profits as a hedge against a rainy day. That's figuratively speaking, of course—it seldom rains in Dell City.

Tascosa, located out in Oldham County, was occupied in the mid-1870s, but civilization caught on at a much later date. Tascosa was held in awe as the toughest town in Texas and probably deserved the recognition. Main Street was lined with dance halls, barrooms, and bawdy houses, and often all three operations flourished under a single roof.

Gunfighters and assorted other toughs partied there, and Billy the Kid was a regular member of the congregation.

Boot Hill Cemetery received the remains of at least twenty-five gun slicks who came out second best in shooting matches.

Additionally, three deputy marshals were terminated in a single day. It was a sad day—one usually lasted a week.

Interplanetary Alliances

When they first ran into each other, Adam was cripping around and complaining about his operation.

"It was worth it though," Eve comforted. "At least for me." That was the first documented spat in the garden, and it was followed by a period of tranquility.

Then Eve heard gossip praising a tree with fruit that was both taste tempting and prohibited by the rules. She beguiled Adam into sharing in the delectables and the blame for the infraction, and for the first time, they detected some differences in their construction. Immediately, they fabricated and slipped into fig leaf raiment.

The landlord dropped by and saw what had been going on, and he stood by his words of warning. Adam and Eve were summarily evicted, and the easy-living period of Earth habitation screeched to a sudden halt.

The frequency of the spats increased, and so too did the intensity, but there were no neighbors to complain about the racket. As a matter of record, there were also periods of domestic tranquility, and unto Adam and Eve two sons were born. They didn't get along even as well as their parents.

In the early 1990s, John Gray, Ph.D. put together a book in hopes of improving communication and successful mergers betwixt the opposing sexes. He titled it *Men Are from Mars, Women Are from Venus*, and it was a smash success and sold like hotcakes.

Mars, Texas, is a crossroads community in Van Zandt County, while Venus is over at the east rim of Johnson County. Venus has the edge in population by a thousand or better and gives credibility to the idea that women outnumber men. Kaufman County is situated between Mars and Venus and may possibly be the sole barrier keeping them from each other's throat.

Anyways, since it has been written in a book, men are from Mars, women are from Venus, and they are both located in Texas.

When a lad from Mars pairs up with a lass from Venus, the Eden Rule comes into play, and they must reside in matrimonial bliss in a location different from their point of origin.

Around the Globe

Most likely it is an unwritten law, but since I was not able to locate it, I've made the decision to ignore the obviously false rumor. Since timidity and proper decorum have always been my short suits, it does not trouble me to confess and crow about my generous contribution to Texas history. I believe it was that artist who did group portraits of soup cans who said that each of us is due "fifteen minutes of fame," or something like that. Mine came with the suddenness of a jet breaking the sound barrier. It was a long time coming and quick to go; howsomever, the experience was semi-great while it lasted. It happened thusly, so brace yourself.

Mrs. Marjorie Morris earned her B.A. and M.A. degrees at North Texas State University and migrated west. She was an English professor at Odessa College for better than two decades, and her consuming interest was the works of Will Shakespeare. As basic training she studied at Yale University, the Folger Shakespeare Library in Washington, D.C., the University of Southern California, and the University of Birmingham in England. Marjorie was bound and determined to ramrod the construction of the most authentic replica of Shakespeare's Theater on Planet Earth, and in Odessa, Texas, which is hard to imagine.

I connected to the teat of GI schooling benefits in the fifties, with the primary aim of knocking down a 140 bucks a month for night attendance at the Odessa College oasis of education. Broadening my horizons with book learning ran a poor second to the money. But Marjorie Morris loomed large as a possible detriment to my garnering of big money in my spare time, since she taught both day and night classes in American, English, and southwestern literature.

To qualify for that fabulous amount of money, it was necessary that I carry the full load (sixteen hours) and maintain a passing grade. Sadly, military adventures had occupied me for several years following high school. In some cases it becomes necessary to resort to falsehood, but when I lie, I've always made it a practice to lie from the heart.

I told Marjorie Morris that I had enjoyed *Romeo and Juliet* a heap more than Mickey Spillane's *Kiss Me Deadly*. As a reward, I was swept into the vortex of creation of the Globe of the Great Southwest, upon the hallowed sands of Odessa College. I became a true believer and worked tirelessly with Marjorie Morris as a co-conspirator. And that 140 bucks arrived like clockwork.

At one point, as the Globe passed the halfway point, the donation flow started to wane, and it was evident that something had to be done. A gala production seemed to be a logical move, so *The Taming of the Shrew* was planned for the courtyard of the Globe. It was a double-barreled extravaganza that we hoped would appeal to the mavens of Will Shakespeare along with the roustabouts, roughnecks, and idiot-spoon operators of the oil leases.

The Drama Department performed the legitimate version as written by Will Shakespeare, and it went off without a hitch and drew thunderous applause from an SRO crowd. Then, the pièce de résistance was unleashed upon that unwary assemblage.

I, with Marjorie's blessing, had written a parody of that immortal work, and after retogging it, the drama group did a rerun in western duds and in cow pasture vernacular. The audience sat in stunned silence throughout the production.

At the tail end of the enactment though, life returned to the ticket buyers.

"Author! Author!" they screamed in unison. "Somebody get a rope!"

I was wise enough to realize that William Shakespeare was not in attendance and mine was the hide in dire jeopardy. Marjorie pointed a trembling finger directly at me. I was away like a shot and cleared the eight-foot masonry wall at a single bound and did not return to classes until after plastic surgery and girth enhancement.

But the fact remaineth and warmeth my feet during the winter season of my dotage. I wrote the first act ever presented at the Globe Theater of the Southwest and lived to tell the story.

The Globe Theater is a viable attraction to the city of Odessa, and Marjorie Morris got it done.

Close Call

Back in the fall of 1985, Russia still decorated its exterior with the Iron Curtain and pushed communism. The United States, of course, was openly critical of most everything Russian at that juncture in history, mainly due to the fact that we were unable to gain a toehold for the expansion of our line of hamburger joints in the land of the star and scythe.

The Russians had numerous missiles with all manner of warheads in place, and they were pointed squarely at the U.S. of A. One press of a button could launch them our way. We countered their fanaticism with patriotism and twice their number of ballistic missiles armed and ready for firing at a moment's notice.

A side game was also being played out in the exploration and exploitation of outer space. They had cosmonauts, while we had astronauts whizzing around through the galaxy claiming uninhabitable orbs of rock for future expansion. When the USA announced that America "was going to hell," the USSR picked up shovels and started digging.

According to the rules of the game, space exploration was conducted on a semihostile basis. One-upmanship was the goal, and competition was keen.

The U.S. astronaut center of operations was down south of Houston, while cosmonaut headquarters were at a secret location somewhere over there, where they get a lot of snow.

Contact between those two entities via the red phone or some such contraption was the norm, and the spokesman for the rivals were in round-the-clock contact, just for safety's sake. Constant access to each other was necessary to avert misunderstandings and fireworks that could easily destroy the world.

In a never-before-released, unedited tape, an incident that could easily have led to Armageddon has been made available on end-of-line dot com. But since you may not be granted access you will be able to read it here.

"Morning, Ivan! How're things going for you this morning?" Houston asked.

"Very well, Tex, thank you. Had a great breakfast of bread and water, and we only got two feet of snow last night," Moscow replied (translated from the Russian).

"Glad to hear it, Ivan. Just want to let you know that the rocket launcher is in place on my console, but I ain't been instructed to push the button yet," Tex said in the West Texas drawl that is recognized all over the civilized world. "Hope you're operating under the same limitation."

"Yes, as far as I know we're not going to launch our rockets today. But, like you, I have the launch control near at hand."

Tex and Ivan lapsed into meaningless conversation at that juncture, and the eight-hour shift for each was off and running just like yesterday, the day before, and, we hoped, the next day.

Suddenly, the sound of revelry at the Houston end became almost deafening, and Ivan inquired as to what the occasion might be.

"We've had an explorer craft out rambling around the galaxy for a good while," Tex explained, "and something remarkable is about to happen."

"Are you allowed to tell me what the occasion might be?" Russia asked.

"We are fixin' to blast off Uranus," Tex chortled with glee.

"Oh, yeah!" Ivan responded with considerable heat. "Well, two can play at the anus blasting game! I'll call my supervisor, and when I get the okay I'll be activating our missiles. It was nice hearing from you."

The superiors of both Tex and Ivan were summoned, took the

phones, and the end of civilization was delayed when those two worthies conferred and worked through the misunderstanding.

It was a close call, and the gravity of the incident was not made public for almost twenty years.

The Mother of All Texas Festivals, 1521

MOTHER OF ALL TEXAS FESTIVALS,
ACT I

August was almighty hot and oppressive back in 1521. Drought conditions were in session, and even the hardy careless weeds lay supine and panting in the blistering sand.

A small band of garishly clad soldiers crept wearily across a merciless expanse. They had not eaten in three days, and water had not passed their parched lips since day before yesterday. Their mood was surly, their visages were clouded, and mutiny was a word being bandied about. They were plumb tuckered out and ready to turn tail and go home. The leader, Ponce by name, was oblivious to the threats and pleadings of his weary troops. Turning back or abandoning the quest for the rumored, wondrous elixir he sought was completely ruled from consideration.

"We shall find the magic waters," Ponce assured his weary troops. "We'll slake our thirst and then claim this whole shebang for our good queen!"

"Bull frog!" muttered the disgruntled troops. "What in tarnation would our queen want with this land? Its only practical use is for filling hour glasses!"

A holy man of Latin derivation staggered and fell to his knees. He was a portly man and was clad in a full-length black robe that absorbed enough heat to bake bread. His function was to provide spiritual guidance and record the exploits of that gallant band, but he'd been ranting in Latin the better part of the week. Since he was the only master of that language in the group, little attention was paid him, and they dismissed his enunciations as the ravings of a lunatic.

He was lifted back to his feet, and the grass burrs and beggar lice were dusted from his sweat-soaked raiment. His eyes stared vacantly, and his swollen tongue protruded through parched lips. It was indeed an unnerving sight.

"Men," Ponce announced, "we're gonna hafta hole up somewhere and stay out of the sun, or we're gonna lose our monk for sure."

They soon located a giant live oak but had to restrain the monk with tethers. He'd gone clean out of his head, and his Latin lamentations were loud and frequent.

The group was in dire straits. From the relative comfort of the shade of that giant oak they could see little except rising heat waves and a few trailing vines in that sea of boiling silica.

Interspersed with the vines were bowling ball–sized globes that were strange and alien to the group. Little interest was paid them except for one soldier's remark that the land looked like "a battlefield plumb full of cannonballs."

"*Citrus vulgaris!*" cried the monk, as he rushed to the limits of his rope and fell to the ground and merciful unconsciousness.

The troops let him lay where he fell, and to a man, they too dominoed and lapsed into troubled sleep.

As the sun disappeared in the west, they roused. Ponce noticed that the holy man had escaped his bonds and was nowhere to be seen. A frantic search revealed only the fact that one soldier's saber was missing.

"He's gone off and done himself in," one hardened veteran muttered, voicing the fear of the entire group.

"Spread out, men," Ponce directed. "We've gotta find him! We're gonna need him to administer last rites if we don't find water soon."

The group fanned out, and it was Ponce who found the monk, sitting in a dense growth of tumbleweed. He sat before a pile of rinds from which he'd devoured the meats of the *citrus vulgaris* he'd pointed out before. He smiled contentedly and patted his belly.

Needless to say, the patch of *citrus vulgaris* (Latin for pie melon) was decimated by that band of soldiers. The group was saved, and they turned and retraced their steps back to the east from whence they came.

Before they left, however, Ponce scratched his family name on a boulder, and a date: August 3, 1521. Beneath the date he affixed a notation. It read: "On this spot, we conducted a *citrus vulgaris* festival."

By now you may have guessed at the implications of this little-known episode in history. Ponce de Leon came to what is now Florida in 1521, with an expedition to colonize that area, but he was also ardently seeking a fountain of youth.

That band took a wrong turn in the Florida panhandle and wound up in what is now Comanche County, Texas. That wrong turn was partially responsible for the naming of a city and marked the very first watermelon slicing to occur on the site of the present celebration, the Peach and Melon Festival.

MOTHER OF ALL TEXAS FESTIVALS,
ACT II

In the autumn of 1806, a baby girl child was born at a Comanche Indian encampment high atop a bluff overlooking the Brazos River in central Texas.

As was the custom back in those days, the father stepped outside the tepee seeking divine inspiration for a suitable name for the infant daughter. He beheld a smoking puddle of liquid near the woodpile and saw a blur of lobo wolf vanish into the saw brier thicket. Satisfied, he went back inside and dubbed his offspring Wolf Flow.

Wolf Flow was a headstrong wench and dealt her parents considerable misery during her formative years. She found fault with Indian ways and lifestyle and had great admiration for the white man. The final shame was administered when she ran off with a shiftless gringo specimen by the name of Leon Noel.

Wolf Flow and Leon settled on the outskirts of San Antonio de Bexar and eked out a precarious survival stealing chickens and newborn piglets.

Unto that union a boy baby was born, and they named him Ed. He wasn't much to look at, but he was a good baby. He never cried. They could even take him along on their fowl filching forays. And did. When Ed turned eleven and still had not made a sound, the parents took notice, but there was nothing to be done. So they didn't.

Following one especially successful night of chicken catching, Leon Noel and Wolf Flow were aroused from their slumber at dawn's early light. Pierre le Croix was banging on their door, and he was one mad Frenchman. Leon shambled outside rubbing sleep from his eyes.

"You have stolen my prize chickens!" Pierre screamed. "I will have my poultry back—and I will have satisfaction for this nefarious deed!" Pierre smote Leon smack across the mouth with a glove. "We will fight the duel!" Pierre screamed.

Leon didn't know any more about duels than he did astronomy, and he stared in befuddlement as Wolf Flow came from the house with a pistol in her hand. Little Ed had roused too and sat trembling under the house with his old yellow dog.

"What might your name be, sir?" Pierre asked.

"Leon Noel," Leon said, "And this here is my woman, Wolf Flow."

"*Sacre bleu!*" Pierre said, "Your names are palindromes." He penciled the names into his duel appointment book.

Leon didn't know what a palindrome was either, but he didn't like the sound of it. He grabbed the pistol from Wolf Flow and shot Pierre graveyard dead on the spot. The neighbors came on the run, and inside of fifteen minutes Leon Noel and Wolf Flow dangled by their respective necks from the limb of a sturdy cottonwood tree.

Little Ed silently shagged it north with his old yellow dog and was never seen again in them parts.

MOTHER OF ALL TEXAS FESTIVALS, ACT III

Ed Noel's banishment from civilized company since his parents were hanged for the execution of M. Pierre le Croix was self-imposed. As a young man he retreated to the wilds of central Texas. His aimless wandering led him, eventually, to a large rock upon which he beheld an unexpected carving. It was his name!

"Sacre bleu!" he must have thought. "Divine fortune has done guided me to the place I belong!" He constructed a rude log cabin with his own hands and a double-bladed ax.

The rock that bore his name was used in the fireplace. Ed lived off the land, much like the Indians of that time. He kept a few chickens, raised a garden, and harvested the bounty of nature. Berries, grapes, persimmons, poke salet and pecans graced his table in their season, and he also partook of deer, squirrel, and swamp-rabbit flesh.

Ed was mute at birth, and that imperfection and his untimely orphanage were the reasons for his flight and hermit existence. The trauma of his childhood drove him from his own kind, but living off the land suited him fine.

Around the first of February in 1836, Ed was sitting in front of his fireplace and a roaring fire. The cabin was warm and snug, and Ed was hulling pecans.

There was a sharp knock upon his door. Warily, Ed crept to a crack he'd purposely left for just such occasions and peered outside. Snow was falling at a terrifying rate, and the temperature was sufficiently frigid to freeze the horns off a brass billy goat. Ed beheld a nearly crazed, half-frozen man there. A spent horse was shivering in the front yard. Even a devout hermit can't turn a man away on such a night, and Ed opened the door and gestured for the stranger to enter.

Gratefully the frigid figure staggered inside, pointing to his ears as he entered.

That stranger was Deaf Smith. He was on a recruiting campaign for General Sam Houston. He'd been crisscrossing central Texas for better than a month trying vainly to scare up an army of volunteers for one of General Sam's pet projects.

Independence from Mexico!

Ed dished Smith a plate of beans and fatback, and as Smith fell upon them victuals, Ed went outside and stabled and hayed Smith's horse.

They sat before the roaring fire far into the night. Smith could not hear, but the talent was of little importance, for Ed Noel could not speak. They gestured amiably and enjoyed a fine evening. Smith would talk, and Ed would nod "yes" or "no," and by this process they communicated with each other, after a fashion.

Next morning the storm had abated, and Smith felt compelled to resume his quest. He thanked Ed for his hospitality, and as he was tightening his cinch, he suddenly realized that he did not know his benefactor's name.

"Can you write your name?" Smith asked.

Ed smiled broadly and nodded his head in the affirmative. He'd spent many a solitary night practicing the printing of his simple name, and he was justly proud that he did not have to sign with an X.

Ed found a piece of paper and the stub of a pencil, sat down, and laboriously lettered his name. Proudly he handed it to Smith. Smith put the paper into his saddlebag and did not remove it until he was back with General Houston.

Upon a map of our future Texas, Deaf Smith pointed out settlements and villages to the good general.

"I want to name this settlement for the man who saved my life," Smith told Sam Houston.

"Fair enough!" the general gestured. "What is his name?" Sam was a master of sign language.

Now Ed Noel had another problem, of which he'd not been able to inform Deaf Smith. As the name was dutifully inscribed on that early map of Texas, no one was aware that Ed Noel was afflicted with dyslexia.

The way he wrote his name looked right to him, but old Ed lettered all words backward. What he actually printed that cold day in February of 1836 is still carried on our maps of today.

"dE leoN" was, of course, what he actually wrote.

And that is the site of the Annual Peach and Melon Festival, which is observed during the first full week in August. The ritual began in 1521 and continues unto this day and time. Admittedly, there was a lengthy skip between Ponce de Leon's inaugural back in 1521 and the modern-day resumption, which now spans eighty-eight years. The De Leon Peach and Melon Festival compares favorably with the Olympic Games, age-wise. And the Olympics also suffered a lengthy gap in continuity.

The Beat Goes On

Virginia was one of the original players. When the renegade thirteen had their falling out with mother England over taxes in 1775, the Old Dominion was willing and able to furnish firebrands for the self-proclaimed United States of America. Virginia's ante of presidents has been seven of the forty-two, and that is the record Texas is edging toward. We didn't even get into the game until 1845 and had to give up republic status as an admission charge.

Dwight D. Eisenhower, a Texan by birth, was Numero Uno Texican to gain lodging at the White House in 1954, and his military expertise enabled him to complete two hitches and quit while he was still winning. He was sixty-three years old, and Texas was 108, at the time. It took awhile to extend the playing field west of the Mississippi and for Texas to master the game.

"Landslide" Lyndon Johnson hit the big time in 1963 when he came off the bench to replace John F. Kennedy. He was reelected in 1964 by a 61–39 percent margin. Lyndon was a by-birth Texan from the wilds of central Texas. He'd had enough by 1969 and didn't try to keep the job.

The third presidential offering was not a cradle Texan, but George Bush, Sr., hung out in these parts and managed to get work as Ronnie Reagan's step-and-fetchit. He was rewarded with the runner-up-to-Ron prize and became the forty-first president of these United States. He managed one term and was ousted by the

wild man from Arkansas—Bill Clinton—who furnished entertainment for the full eight-year term limit.

Reminiscent of tag team wrasslin', George W. Bush was encouraged and abetted by Daddy Bush, generous contributors, brother Jeb, and the Supreme Court in his campaign to bestow compassionate conservatism upon the U.S. of A. and the rest of the civilized world, with the notable exception of the "Axis of Evil."

He's already being lauded for a second term, and his "war chest" is probably all swole up, even though ENRON has fallen upon hard times.

In a nutshell, Texas has now furnished four starters as quarterback for America the Beautiful. And if glowing polls continue above 50 percent, we have a good shot at keeping W on the job for a full eight years.

That failing, Texas might elect to go to Plan B for another gain on Virginia in total head count. They're in the lead by a seven-to-four margin, but you've got to remember, they had a sixty-year head start in the Presidential Derby, and it ain't only the Texas males they need to watch.

Miriam "Ma" Amanda Wallace Ferguson took control of the office of Texas governor when her husband James Edward was impeached on some kind of honesty technicality in 1925, and she served that term and was reelected to a full four-year term.

Governor Ann Richards, a Harley Davidson–fancying kind of gal, sat high in the saddle from 1991 until 1995, so you can readily see that Texas women are feisty enough to take the reins if they see an opening.

Since George W. Bush was also governor of Texas, it's likely that he and his wife mate, Laura, read up on the coup of Ma and Pa Ferguson and may have found comfort in the incident. And there ain't no reason to exclude its working on a national level. Actually, Laura might be the better president of the two. She knows enough to chew a pretzel before she swallows it.

As the world turns on the days of our lives, you can bet your boots that folks are going to be interested in knowing who Texas is warming up in the bullpen.

And they'd be well advised to check the cowpen once in awhile, too.

Aftword

The Lone Star State originated with a baptism by fire. Self-proclaimed Texians took a lungful of air when they congregated, faced the superior numbers of a tyrant country, and dared to gamble their lives for freedom from oppression and go for independence.

The Republic of Texas went it alone with a ragtag army of volunteers and amazed the world and their adversaries to achieve statehood in the United States of America. There were no Texan laggards in the War between the States, and they followed their conscience in standing up for the ones who brung them to the dance. And the final battle of the Civil War was fought on Texas soil. Even though that war had officially ended, the Texas troops won that final battle.

Texas has ever positioned itself on the cutting edge when America marches off to war, and it is unlikely that they will ever change their ways.

When America was attacked by the Empire of Japan in 1941, Texas's response was instantaneous.

A greater percentage of Texans than citizens of any other state answered the call and served in the armed services. Three quarters of a million young men and women served in the Army, Navy, Marines, Air Force, or the Coast Guard.

Almost eight thousand Texas daughters served in the Women's Army Corps, and another four thousand did duty in the Women Accepted for Volunteer Emergency Service, the Coast Guard, and in the Marines.

More than fifteen thousand Texans lost their lives in World War II in the army, mostly in combat. Yet another seven thousand laid down their lives in other branches of the service.

Thirty-six Texans earned the Congressional Medal of Honor, and another ten won the navy's Medal of Honor. The most decorated soldier was a rural Texas lad from Farmersville. His name was Audie Murphy. The navy's most decorated was Samuel D. Dealey, who called Dallas home.

There were 135 Texans who wore the rank of general, and one, Dwight Eisenhower, was the Supreme Allied Commander in Europe. He was born in Denison.

Twelve Texans advanced to the rank of admiral in the navy, and Chester Nimitz of Fredericksburg was commander of the Pacific Fleet.

Oveta Culp Hobby was the colonel who headed up the Women's Army Corps, and she too was a Texan.

The Thirty-Sixth Division was the first American force to land on the European continent, at Salerno, Italy, and it fought its way through Italy, France, Germany, and Austria in a four-hundred-day campaign. The Lone Star Flag of Texas was carried alongside Old Glory. The Thirty-Sixth was predominately made up of Texans and was often referred to as the Texas Army.

Texans have never backed down from a fight, and the unwritten motto must surely be the quoted advice of David Crockett who died at the Alamo: "Be sure you're right—then go ahead."

With hat in hand, I ask forgiveness for my tacky behavior when the list of volunteer Texans who served in roles as presidents of the republic and as governors of Texas was printed back yonder as a puzzle. Repentance is chicken soup for the soul, and despite my hesitancy in listing the correct solution to the dignitary and birth origin, I hereby submit the facts:

Presidents	*Birthplace*
David G. Burnet	New Jersey
Sam Houston	Virginia
Mirabeau B. Lamar	Georgia
Anson Jones	Iowa

Governors

J. Pickney Henderson	North Carolina
George T. Wood	Georgia
Peter Hansbrough Bell	Virginia
J. W. Henderson	Tennessee
Elisha M. Pease	Connecticut
Hardin R. Runnels	Mississippi
Edward Clark	Georgia
Francis R. Lubbock	South Carolina
Fletcher S. Stockdale	Kentucky
Andrew J. Hamilton	Alabama
James W. Throckmorton	Tennessee
Edmund J. Davis	Florida
Richard Coke	Virginia
Richard B. Hubbard	Georgia
Oran M. Roberts	South Carolina
John Ireland	Connecticut
Lawrence Sullivan Ross	Iowa
Charles A. Culberson	Alabama
Joseph Sayers	Mississippi
S. W. T. Lanham	South Carolina
Oscar Branch Colquitt	Georgia
W. Lee O'Daniel	Ohio
George W. Bush	Connecticut

Now I feel better. My conscience and sinuses are clear.